DUDEVOTIONAL

Vol. 1

DUDEVOTIONAL
Vol. 1

meditations
on total
badassery
and other
masculine
stuff

ANDY PARKER

Soul
Reno
Media

Published by Soul Reno Media

ISBN 978-1-966574-16-3 (paperback)

To every man who wants to be a better man.

Contents

Also by Andy Parker

Books

I Don't Really Care, Margaret: The Re-Election of Trump and the Return of the Patriarchy

Gentlemen, This is the Gospel

Make Patriarchy Great Again: A Guide to Save the World

Renovating the Soul: Meditations on Christ and Life from a Serial Renovator

Commentaries

God's Gonna Cut You Down: Meditations on the Book of Nahum

Farther Along: Meditations on the Book of Ecclesiastes

I Will Wait for Him: Meditations on the Book of Habakkuk

I Fled Him: Meditations on the Book of Jonah

Journals

The Christmas Journal: Let Earth Receive Her King

The Holiness Journal: Strive Towards Holiness, Without Which No One Will See the Lord

The Gratitude Journal: Praise God from Whom All Blessings Flow

Introduction

"We need the iron qualities that go with true manhood. We need the positive virtues of resolution, of courage, of indomitable will, of power to do without shrinking the rough work that must always be done."

Theodore Roosevelt

Every which way you look, men are getting kicked in the balls. Mocked, maligned, and manipulated by the media. Made a cuckold by culture, and prostituted and prostrated by politicians and pastors alike. For well over a decade masculinity has been proclaimed to be toxic by our secular pundits, professors, and prophets.

Men are so despised that the intelligentsia has deemed them too dangerous to even get started. As soon as they hit the public prison, I mean educational system, they are told to act like little girls, and if they don't comply, they are hit with a chemical cocktail to force it upon them. Worse yet, if they can brainwash them to the point of breaking, they will cut their balls off before they drop and pump them full of puberty blockers and lady hormones.

Despite this bleak and barren picture of butchered boys and malnourished and feminized men, there are signs of hope. Men are waking up to the play that has been run on them by politicians who fear them and want to control them, pastors who don't know what to do with them, and women who want to be them. However, the tides are beginning to change, and men are hearing a clarion call deep down in their masculine soul to rise up and act like men.

Perhaps one of the most encouraging things over the last several years has been the rate at which young men are red pilling. They want to pick up the mantle of the glad assumption of sacrificial responsibility and count themselves among the hall of great men that have gone before them. They want to get married and make babies, lots of them. They want to work hard and have dominion—guarding, keeping, protecting, creating, building, conquering, and so on. They want to live a life that matters, and amen to that! They want to free the church from its femmie captivity and rescue our nation from politicians of both parties that are about as upright as soft-serve ice cream in Mississippi in July.

Men are beginning to crawl out of the pit of egalitarianism and smash the shackles of soft complementarianism that have enslaved them for so long. They are beginning to see their role in God's economy as image bearers and stewards of our Great King. They are beginning to understand that they have been cut from royal cloth, set apart by God to rule over creation as godly men and patriarchs. This is all fantastic news that will usher in generational change.

If we truly want to see Christ glorified in our lives, and we want to see our wives flourish and our children's children's children prosper, it will require us to make sacrifices and bear the brunt of the load. This is all good news because we are men, and we like work, and because God gave us broad shoulders for a reason. So knuckle up, buttercup, because the road ahead is going to be scrappy.

However, this great endeavor, this great adventure, this great mission that is before us will not be easy. We will face opposition without and within. Without, because snakes usually do not go gentle into that good night, and they certainly do not like relinquishing power. Within, not only because we need to wage war against the temptations and desires of the flesh so that we can be upright men of character, but also because many of us are men raised by women. This is not a jab at women; it is to simply state the obvious: women can't raise men to be men.

Many of us are picking up the pieces of a broken past and trying to be good men in a broken world but often feel like a ship at sea without a rudder or a compass. I am well acquainted with this feeling, and I understand you. Even more important than this is that God the Father knows and understands exactly where you are at. God is a good Father, and there is hope, and by His grace there will be generational change in our homes and through our lineage.

The way forward is simple, not easy but simple. Humble yourself and be fathered by God through His word and prayer. Becoming a good man begins by submitting yourself to the Father through Christ. Pour into your wife and children; this is the best investment you will ever make in your life. Find a good church that breathes fire and a band of brothers that will encourage you and bust your balls. All of this will take time; don't rush it. You don't sprint up a mountain; you take it one step at a time. Pray a lot and then some more.

Also, find good books written by men for men that will encourage and challenge you to be a better man. This is where I hope this book fits in your life. Guys really don't need much. They need some encouragement and to be challenged towards growth, or if you prefer, to have their balls busted from time to time. I have tried to accomplish both with this book.

I have compiled some of the coolest *dude* poems written, and though this is by no means exhaustive, I tried to be reader sensitive with length, knowing that most men probably aren't into reading poems, especially long ones. The one exception is an excerpt from *Man in the Arena*, which is included because it's awesome. All these poems are pithy, memorable, and masculine and provide wonderful examples, illustrations, and word pictures of masculine virtues. The reflections that follow, when meditated upon and put into practice in your life, by God's grace will help you to be a better man and a more complete dude as you get after it!

In short, this is a resource that will aid you in your quest of mastering the art of badassery and other masculine stuff.

You're welcome & cheers!

Andy

The Man in the Arena

The Man in the Arena

"It is not the critic who counts: not the man who points out how the strong man stumbles or where the doer of deeds could have done better. The credit belongs to the man who is actually in the arena, whose face is marred by dust and sweat and blood, who strives valiantly, who errs and comes up short again and again, because there is no effort without error or shortcoming, but who knows the great enthusiasms, the great devotions, who spends himself in a worthy cause; who, at the best, knows, in the end, the triumph of high achievement, and who, at the worst, if he fails, at least he fails while daring greatly, so that his place shall never be with those cold and timid souls who knew neither victory nor defeat."

Theodore Roosevelt

"The Man in the Arena" is a small excerpt from a much larger speech given by Teddy Roosevelt called "Citizenship in a Republic," delivered at the Sorbonne, in Paris, France, on April 23rd, 1910. The whole speech is good, but this one paragraph is gold and perfectly encapsulates what Teddy would call the "strenuous life." Not only that, but this one little paragraph also touches a nerve and a desire deep down in the masculine soul. That is, to be a *man in the arena.*

At rock bottom, there are basically two types of men: those in the arena engaged in the battles of life and those who are disengaged spectators in the stadium who criticize the actions of others with puritanical zeal. Though these fastidious crusaders have never taken any of the actions or risks they so freely and unreservedly criticize, nor will they ever, they are thoroughly convinced that they would do it better.

"The Man in the Arena" is a perfect example of man and message blending in perfect harmony. Of course, the words have weight in and of themselves and surely resonate with every man that doesn't sit down to pee. However, the man can make or break or substantiate or completely discredit the message. For example, no one is going to listen to dietary advice from someone who looks like they ate a small village, nor marriage advice from someone who has been divorced multiple times, nor parenting advice from the childless, nor advice on masculinity from a Democrat.

Say whatever you want about Teddy's politics, personality, or place in history—sure, all of that is fair game; however, the one thing that cannot be denied is that he truly was a man in the arena, he truly embodied the strenuous life, or, if you will, he was a total badass. If you doubt me on this one, let's briefly compare resumes. Before he turned fifty, he served in the New York legislature, was the under-secretary in the Navy, a police commissioner, the governor of New York, the vice president and the president of the United States. He was an author, reporter, editor, and journalist; ran his own cattle ranch; founded the Rough Riders; conducted expeditions on four continents; read a book a day for most of his life; and was a devoted family man who raised his six children.

Teddy's stories are the stuff of legend, whether it was riding a bull moose or getting shot in the chest and then going on to speak for an hour after that. Not to mention he is still the only president to set up a boxing ring in the White House so he could spar with the heavyweight champion of the world. That's just the beginning of Teddy's lure, all of which was made possible because he was a man who practiced what he preached. He was a man who truly embodied the strenuous life. He was truly a man in the arena, grinding, struggling, fighting, enduring, and overcoming.

It is important to note that this level of badassery isn't something that you are born with. No, this level of badassery must be forged in the fiery hot furnace of trials, hardships, heartache, and good old-fashioned pain. Though Teddy was born into a wealthy New York family, he certainly wasn't born with anything that resembled physical prowess, or, if you prefer a more modern designation, privilege. As a child he was weak and frail and stricken with debilitating asthma. Many doctors thought that he was destined to be housebound his whole life.

After trying every form of therapy available at the time and failing to make any progress, Teddy's father sat down with his son. As the story goes, the father told his son that he had the mind but not the body; however, without his body, his mind would never go as far as it could. He told his young boy how difficult it was going to be to make his body strong, but that he knew he could do it. Teddy looked at his father and told him he would do it, and the amazing thing is, he did.

Proverbs 20:21 says, "An inheritance gained hastily in the beginning will not be blessed in the end." There is an important lesson here for us in a world now filled with performance-enhancing drugs and Ozempic. Any real lasting change that not only shapes the body but also your character that is forged through hard work and suffering over extended periods of time requires you to be consistent and to grind. Teddy transformed himself through raw determination, devotion, and discipline. He forced himself through hours of grueling exercises every day for well over a decade before he started to see real change in his health, which occurred when he was a freshman in college.

We often like to think that our trials in life will be a one and done, in that this was a trial we suffered through, and we learned what we needed to learn, and now we can live happily ever after believing we never need to go through trials ever again. However, that is not how God works in the arena of our lives. The trials that we go through strengthen us to endure greater trials. Such was the case with Teddy.

On February 14, 1884, Teddy endured an unimaginable loss. His wife had a rough pregnancy but was able to deliver a healthy baby girl. However, she suffered from Bright's disease and within a short time after the delivery grew increasingly ill. Teddy was called home to be with his dying wife. As if this wasn't bad enough, his mother had also fallen ill with the final stages of typhoid. Both women lay dying in the same house at the same time. He divided his time going back and forth between rooms trying to comfort his dying wife and mother. His mother died at midnight, his wife dying the following afternoon. After enduring the double funeral of his wife and mother, his daughter was baptized in the same church the following day.

Broken by grief, he needed to get away. He needed to get alone with God in the wilderness. He needed physical hardship to take his mind away from the pain and suffering. He sent his daughter to be cared for by his sister; he sold almost everything he had and moved to the Dakotas to a cattle ranch for three years. Comfort would not help him. He needed discomfort and hardship, he needed to overcome, and he needed to remember what dominion looked like.

These three years were formative in Teddy's life. Not only did he overcome the wilderness, but he also overcame himself, creating a bold and fearless confidence that would follow him the rest of his life. James says, "Count it all joy, my brothers, when you meet trials of various kinds, for you know that the testing of your faith produces steadfastness. And let steadfastness have its full effect, that you may be perfect and complete, lacking in nothing." (Jam. 1:2-4).

Not only are trials, suffering, and hardship a part of life, but they are also a sign of life. G.K. Chesterton once said, "A dead thing can go with the stream, but only a living thing can go against it." There is a reason why we don't remember critics. They don't have lives any of us want or aspire to. You should never take life advice from someone who has a life you wouldn't advise. This is why the critic doesn't count, and this is why they criticize the man in the arena. The man in the arena is a constant reminder of everything the critic is not. The man in the arena is a doer, a man of action. The critic is simply a talker. Regardless of how many times you may stumble, or where your actions could be done better, you will always be further ahead than the critic.

The man in the arena is striving for a goal, while the critic simply ridicules the way he strives while accomplishing nothing himself. Let them talk; the critic doesn't count because he only talks about the one doing the doing while actually doing nothing. It is far better to stumble and learn as you go. It is better to be marred in dust and sweat and blood than to talk about the ones who are.

To come up short again and again and again is proof you're still in the game, still striving, still fighting, still alive. Not only is this a sign of life, but to strive with great enthusiasm and great devotion and to empty oneself for a worthy cause is great gain even in loss. Again, to quote Chesterton, "The one perfectly divine thing, the one glimpse of God's paradise given on earth, is to fight a losing battle—and not lose it."

As Christians we live through dying, we gain through loss, and we are filled by being empty; therefore, nothing should stop us from stepping into the fray. We are not descendants of fearful men, nor are we of timid stock. God has given us His Spirit, which is not a spirit of fear, but rather of power, love, and self-control. If you're afraid of stumbling, if you're afraid of not measuring up, if you're afraid of the dust, sweat, and blood, if you're afraid of the loss and the pain and the trials, be afraid and go anyway. Go into the colosseum of life and rub some dirt in your hands like Maximus Decimus Meridius and get after it. The secret is that even to fail while daring greatly is victory.

Life is filled with pain, sorrow, trials, and failure. If you are getting after it, you're going to fail, and you're going to fail, and you're going to fail, and you're going to come up short again and again and again. And then you're going to win. At the end of all the hurt, hard work, striving, and battle, you will know more about the world, yourself, and Christ than the critic will ever know. So then, Gladiator, go and get your hands dirty!

Nations Are Built by Men

A Nation's Strength

What makes a nation's pillars high
And its foundations strong?
What makes it mighty to defy
The foes that round it throng?

It is not gold. Its kingdoms grand
Go down in battle shock;
Its shafts are laid on sinking sand,
Not on abiding rock.

Is it the sword? Ask the red dust
Of empires passed away;
The blood has turned their stones to rust,
Their glory to decay.

And is it pride? Ah, that bright crown
Has seemed to nations sweet;
But God has struck its luster down
In ashes at his feet.

Not gold but only men can make
A people great and strong;
Men who for truth and honor's sake
Stand fast and suffer long.

Brave men who work while others sleep,

Who dare while others fly...
They build a nation's pillars deep
And lift them to the sky.

Ralph Waldo Emerson

The very first words of the Bible are, "In the beginning, God created the heavens and the earth." (Gen. 1:1). It should not surprise us then that the first Christian creed, the Apostles' Creed, includes this truth as the first fundamental statement of faith, "I believe in God, the Father Almighty, creator of heaven and earth." Creation is a trinitarian masterpiece. God the Father created through Jesus Christ, by the power of the Holy Spirit. It pleased God to create all things, visible and invisible. He did this to manifest the glory of His power, goodness, and wisdom.

The reality of God being our Creator is familiar enough. Perhaps, it's even too familiar, so much so that we rarely stop to consider the profundity of that, and when we do, it is usually in relationship to His power. No doubt we should consider that He is the Almighty after all, but just think of the creativity, complexity, beauty, and wonder of it all.

He created everything, all of it. It isn't just that God created the seas and everything therein. He created the sound and feel of the waves slowly rippling in on a hot sunny day. He created the taste of the salty air and the smell of slightly burned skin. He created the multitudinous colors in the sky as the sun sets over the Arizona desert. He created what freshly fallen snow would look like over the Colorado mountains. He created what puppies would smell like and what a baby's laughter would sound like. The list is literally endless. The depth of the riches of wisdom and knowledge of God are beyond searching out.

On the sixth day of creation, at the culmination of God's creative work, He made man in His image and after His likeness. Man is not only the only copy creature in all of creation, but as an image bearer, he is also a re-creator. Together with his wife, they are to be fruitful and multiply, filling the earth and subduing it. Man's mission is to be creaturely recreative; he is to have dominion over all things to the glory of God. Certainly this includes the glories of marriage and children, but also working with mind and hands. We mimic our Father in heaven. We create, we build, we cultivate; it is our nature as men.

We look for frontiers to explore; no depth is too deep, no height too high, and no length too far. We long to search out and to know. We actively seek out the wilderness, with its mysteries and its dangers. We seek to conquer, overcome, and tame. There is a reason why little boys build forts and can make a weapon out of any stick. They know the world is not only filled with possibilities and obstacles that must be overcome but also with dragons that must be defeated. One day they will grow to be men, and by God's grace they will remember that they are from royal stock and will once again experience the joy they had in the backyard defending their little kingdom they built.

Men were made to have dominion. Men were made to rule and to build, create, expand, cultivate, and conquer. One may state with puritanical fervor that women do the same, and certainly they do, but they do so as women and not as men. I know it seems utterly radical and revolutionary to state the most obvious of things today, so let me take the opportunity to state what we have always known: men and women are different. Profound, right? Not really! In fact, it is the most obvious of obvious things. Most parents, before their beautiful little babies are born, want to know the sex—boy or girl. One may say, "Well, that's just plumbing and doesn't determine the gender of the child." To which we would respond with, "Dear sir or madame, you are a retard!"

The plumbing is designed by God, and that plumbing runs all the way down and all the way through. We are different and complementary in every respect, by design, and what God has designed is good. At this point, it is not uncommon to hear some manner of protestation among the intelligentsia among us about anomalies and such. No doubt those exist, but that does nothing but prove the point; they are anomalies after all. We are all aware of the butch chick and the soft dude. In a bygone era, we would have been able to tell one to act like a lady and the other to act like a man. Not only would that have been considered good, but everyone would have known what you meant. The secret is, those words still mean what they meant 100 years ago; the only thing that has changed is our affinity for the obvious.

God gave men inquisitive, sharp minds and broad shoulders for a reason. It wasn't just to fend off predators, but it was to tame the wilderness and bring order out of chaos. This order isn't just order in a wooden sense, but man desires to make it all lovely and good. All one has to do is open their eyes and look around. Every house, every church, every school, and every public building has been built by men. Think of the skylines of every major city in our country. All of those massive structures of concrete and steel were designed and built by men. We've all seen the old black and white photos of men walking around on steel beams hundreds of feet in the air without any protection or safety standards. Why would they do that? Because they are men, and that's what we do.

Think of the massive and productive farms that fill our land. At one point they were bare fields, and now they are fruitful crops in abundance. If anyone has seen the hands of an old farmer, they are like worn leather—the badge of honor from decades of hard work. Will they ever ask for a thank you? No. Why? Because they are men, and that's not what we do. And it's not just the grit of the men willing to do the hard manual labor; it's also the engineering, design, building, and operating of the machinery that works the land. Also the steel and petroleum needed for such work are, again, all engineered, retrieved, and harvested by men.

There are those today that declare and decry that the strength of men is aggressive, oppressive, and violent. This is remarkably stupid. It is true that every strength and gift can be abused and misused, but all one needs to do is not only look down the annals of time to see that this is untrue; they just need to look around today. Almost everything we enjoy was formulated in the minds of men and built off the backs of men.

Great nations are built the same way homes, churches and businesses are—built by men. "Men who for truth and honor's sake / Stand fast and suffer long. / Brave men who work while others sleep, / Who dare while others fly..." (lines 19-22). Everything good—homes, churches, businesses, nations, and empires—was built by men with mouths to feed. This is why it is so foolish to disparage men or to think that the exalting of men and masculinity is somehow disparaging of women. Actually, the exact opposite is true. Why do men desire to do such things? Why did God wire them in such a way? Man's fruitfulness and productivity are directed towards woman.

All of the labor, hard work, responsibility, and sacrifice are taken on because man desires to bless those under his care, those whom he is responsible for. Man desires to take all God has given him and give it to his children better. He wants to take them further up and further in—further out and further onward. It is for the love of those behind him that man looks outward and upward.

The height of the skyline is determined by the depth of the footings. Love Jesus, fear God, and keep His commandments, and pour deeply into your home, repent daily, pray often, dream big, and go build!

God, Give Us Men!

GOD, give us men!
A time like this demands
Strong minds, great hearts, true faith and ready hands;
Men whom the lust of office does not kill;
Men whom the spoils of office can not buy;
Men who possess opinions and a will;
Men who have honor; men who will not lie;
Men who can stand before a demagogue
And damn his treacherous flatteries without winking!
Tall men, sun-crowned, who live above the fog
In public duty, and in private thinking;
For while the rabble, with their thumb-worn creeds,
Their large professions and their little deeds,
Mingle in selfish strife, lo! Freedom weeps,
Wrong rules the land and waiting Justice sleeps.

Josiah Gilbert Holland

There is an old saying. Well, I don't know how old it actually is, but there is a saying. No one believes that masculinity is toxic when shit hits the fan. Something like this usually pops up on a great multitude of memes after a tragedy or natural disaster, accompanied by a picture of a normal everyday man carrying a woman, child, or even animals out of flood zones or collapsed buildings and the like. And everyone knows that a few rednecks with a pickup truck and a tow chain are going to be there to help before any government assistance arrives.

The fact of the matter is we need men. In fact, the strength of any nation is determined by the strength of the men that make it up. Therefore, any people or nation that marginalize, mock, malign, and seek to manipulate the men are in for a rude awakening because such will also occur upon the nation. That is, the nation will soon find itself marginalized, mocked, maligned, and manipulated not only from without but also from within. You can't hate half your population and think they are toxic without some pretty cataclysmic consequences. One has to seriously question the integrity of a marriage if they see both spouses wearing shirts with the saying written on them, "I'm with stupid."

Such is the case with our nation. We have been force-fed piles of horse shit in the form of DEI, like a toddler forced to eat its veggies. This has been orchestrated by the malevolence of the race-commies, the homo-commies, the tranny-commies, and your everyday run-of-the-mill commie-

commies. This has all been done with the intent of weakening and emasculating the men. Why? Because raw, masculine strength will always be a threat to weak hegemonic despots who desperately want power but whom no man (the anatomically correct kind) will follow…think of men like Bill Gates, Barack Obama, Russel Moore, and Rosie O'Donnell.

C.S. Lewis once said, "Of all tyrannies, a tyranny sincerely exercised for the good of its victims may be the most oppressive. It would be better to live under robber barons than under omnipotent moral busybodies." We've been led for some time by omnipotent moral busybodies that have been trying to reshape the world into their own androgynous image, and it's disgusting. The result of which has been terrible on men, women, and children. Men were made to be protector-providers, and when you rob them of this, you leave them at sea like a ship with a rudder and with no sail and no map—without direction or purpose. However, there is always porn, prescription drugs, and PlayStation to help pacify and placate the pain.

Omnipotent moral busybodies have been telling us for decades that there are no differences between men and women and that women can do everything that men can do, which is exactly why physical standards must be lower for women regarding any protector role. Does anyone actually believe we are any better off as a result of all of this madness? If you were in a life-threatening situation and needed to call the police and an overweight DEI lady cop showed up, would you be comforted?

Just think of the Secret Service detail that was assigned to President Trump the day he was shot at in Butler, Pennsylvania.

The reason we got that iconic fist-pump "fight, fight, fight" photo was because the woman in front of him was too small to cover him. Sure the photo was cool, but when we see it, we should be reminded that if there was another shooter, he would have been dead. Or think of the Secret Service agent that was unable to holster her weapon under pressure. She looks like the only time she runs is to the border for some Taco Bell.

Some may read that last statement and think maybe I went too far. Actually, I haven't gone far enough. Men are to be the protectors. They are wired this way not just through physical strength but also mental strength. And when you throw women into these roles to show how enlightened we are, we soon find out that the mercies of the wicked are cruel because people get hurt. If you still think I am being a jerk, let me ask you this: if your house was burning and your children were stuck inside and a fire truck showed up with all women, would you be comforted or terrified? If your children died, would you still be virtue signaling?

I don't know who originally said it, but it rings true: "Hard times create strong men. Strong men create good times. Good times create weak men. And weak men create hard times." We are living in a time of weak men and hard times. The irony is that we've gotten to this point, a point where we can bash on men because we've grown too comfortable, overindulgent, and apathetic because of the good times created by strong men.

One may argue that men use their strength to oppress and abuse and that this must be stopped. To which we would respond with, "Yes, and how do you propose to do that?" Through the strength of women, or through weak, passive-aggressive, effeminate men like those mentioned above? Either option creates far more harm. The only thing that corrects and rectifies said abuses are righteous men who use their strength to build up what is good and tear down what is wicked.

A time like ours demands strong men. As Holland said above, "A time like this demands / Strong minds, great hearts, true faith and ready hands; / Men whom the lust of office does not kill; / Men whom the spoils of office cannot buy; / Men who possess opinions and a will; / Men who have honor; men who will not lie; / Men who can stand before a demagogue / And damn his treacherous flatteries without winking!" (lines 2-9).

These words help to put masculine strength into perspective. Being strong is much more than being physically strong, although that never hurts. To be strong is to act like a man. It is to have a resiliency of spirit. Strength is the ability to endure under or resist pressure. Weight training is called resistance training for a reason.

Therefore, to be strong as a man means being able to endure under the pressures of life and press ahead. It means to push back against resistance. We would describe this kind of man as resolute, resilient, upright, and immoveable. God gave men broad shoulders because He intends for them to carry a load. This can take on multiple forms, and strength is required for all of it.

Strength is needed to resist the omnipotent moral busybodies of our day. Strength is needed to resist the lust and spoils of office. Strength is needed to press forward despite the many dangers ahead. Strength is needed to exercise the physical and spiritual discipline necessary to be a better man. Strength is needed to confront the evils of our day. Strength is needed to build and have dominion. Strength is needed to endure a struggling marriage and come out the other side better. Strength is needed to endure the trials and tragedies of life. Strength is needed to stand upright when all others are cowed to oppressive powers. Strength is needed to step into the arena of life come what may. Strength is needed to get up and get after it day after day after day.

This world needs strong men. Men who see their role as protector-provider as God-given, and because it is God-given, it is God-directed. This means that masculine strength should be used to build up that which is good, beautiful, and true and tear down what is wicked and false. Masculine strength is God-given, and when it is God-directed, it should never be apologized for, and as we look around at the state of things, perhaps we may say that it has never been more needed. Your home requires your strength. Your church and community require your strength. Your nation requires your strength. Therefore, act like a man and be strong.

CHARACTER

A Man

A man doesn't whine at his losses,
A man doesn't whimper and fret,
Or rail at the weight of his crosses
And ask life to rear him a pet.
A man doesn't grudgingly labor
Or look upon toil as a blight;
A man doesn't sneer at his neighbor
Or sneak from a cause that is right.
A man doesn't sulk when another
Succeeds where his efforts have failed;
Doesn't keep all his praise for the brother
Whose glory is publicly hailed;
And pass by the weak and the humble
As though they were not of his clay;
A man doesn't ceaselessly grumble
When things are not going his way.
A man looks on woman as tender
And gentle, and stands at her side
At all times to guard and defend her,
And never to scorn or deride.
A man looks on life as a mission.
To serve, just so far as he can;
A man holds his noblest ambition
On earth is to live as a man.

Edgar Guest

Men are not *the* problem, despite what our modern-day prophets of tolerance would have you believe. However, men can still be *a* problem, but so too can women. The problem here lies not in God's good creation. The problem is with a perversion of God's good creation. Sin is the problem. When men use all of their strength and God-given desire for dominion in a selfish and destructive way, it's bad all around, and there is no way around that one. It's just bad. However, even in an age drowning in the femmie zeitgeist, we still know the opposite is true. That is, men who are sacrificial and responsible and use their strength to build in constructive ways are good for everyone, especially women and children.

Saying that we need good men didn't used to be controversial, not at all. When Bonnie Tyler sang "Holding Out for a Hero," nobody thought she was stupid or misguided until recently. I would argue that despite all of our egalitarian bluster and bravado, we still secretly agree with Bonnie. Nobody is holding out for a butch dyke that identifies as a man. Despite the similarity in appearance, everyone knows deep down in their bones that Wendy and Bob the Builder are different. This difference runs all the way down to their bones, of which their DNA will attest.

Now we come to a very important distinction that must be made, which may cause a gender-gestapo brain-bleed. That is, the biological difference that runs all the way down through our bones is something that should be evident in our lives. Here is the big idea: everyone that comes into the world is either born a male or female—mind blown, I know. But this is where we come to the rub in the road.

If you are born a male, you were created to grow and mature into a particular thing. That particular thing is a man. Now, one may quip, doesn't that happen through natural processes? Meaning, all one has to do to become a man is live long enough. No doubt we do use this word this way. However, we also use this term in a completely different way, in that if I were to look at an adult male and say, "That's not a man," even in our confused culture, you would know exactly what I mean.

In this example, what is actually being said? We are saying that this adult male does not exhibit characteristics of what a man should be; he is not acting like a man. So then, to be a man is more than just anatomy and biology. It is the proper exercise and manifestation of God-designed male anatomy and biology. This is what we would call masculinity, and masculinity properly exercised is what we would rightly call being a man.

Just as a side note, this is where the term "toxic masculinity" is not only misguided but also destructive. What is actually being identified as toxic is sin, not masculinity per se. Just because a man sins doesn't make masculinity any more toxic than if a woman were to sin, which would then make femininity toxic. Surprisingly, no one is arguing for that, which gives us a clue as to what is actually going on here. If masculinity is the proper exercise and manifestation of what God designed males to be—namely men—then calling masculinity toxic is really a backdoor way of redesigning what God created as good.

Before King David died, he gave these parting words to his son Solomon, who would rule in his place: "When David's time to die drew near, he commanded Solomon his son, saying, 'I am about to go the way of all the earth. Be strong, and show yourself a man, and keep the charge of the LORD your God, walking in his ways and keeping his statutes, his commandments, his rules, and his testimonies, as it is written in the Law of Moses, that you may prosper in all that you do and wherever you turn,…" (1 Kings 2:1-3).

Be strong and show yourself a man. He wasn't telling his son to be a male; he was telling him to act like it. Show yourself to be a man. What does that mean? Well, it means to be strong and to keep the charge of the Lord, walking in His ways and keeping His statutes, commandments, rules, and testimonies. This life will test you over and over and over again. To be a man is to face it all with a godly resolve and to do so even with joy, knowing what is being produced in you as a result, namely character. Paul says, "Not only that, but we rejoice in our sufferings, knowing that suffering produces endurance, and endurance produces character, and character produces hope," (Romans 5:3-4).

Therefore, when we say that someone is *a man*, we are saying much more than that they are a grown male who looks the part. We are saying this guy is growing into what God designed him to be. Internally, something is different about him. His bones have been refined by the fiery forge of life.

He has been tested and endured, and that endurance has produced character. A man knows who he is before the Lord and tackles life head-on. He doesn't whine, or whimper, or rail against the weight of his crosses, nor does he need a therapy hamster to get through life. Life is challenging and very difficult at times. Not only does creation groan under the weight of sin, making hard work harder, but it is filled with dragons and deceivers that seemingly lurk around every corner. It is the joy and duty of a man to do the work, slay the dragon, and shine light on the deceivers.

A man doesn't look down upon his neighbor, nor does he look to cut corners. Doing what is right is right for its own sake because it is pleasing to the Lord, regardless of anyone noticing. He is able to give another man his due for his success regardless of that man's tribe or creed. Give credit where credit is due, and if you don't like it, then work harder and figure it out, but you don't begrudge another man for his success.

A man should hunger and thirst for righteousness, do justice and love kindness, and walk humbly with God. He should not look down on those who are less fortunate than him but should have compassion on them, knowing full well that if it was not for the grace of God, his conditions would be the same, if not worse. A man doesn't grumble, complain, or scoff at difficult times or failures but learns from them, knowing that failure is not final and that no education is free.

A man knows his place in God's kingdom as a redeemed image bearer through Christ. Seeking to be more and more like Jesus in true knowledge, righteousness, and holiness, walking in the fear of the Lord. His mission is dominion beginning in his home with the way that he loves, guards, protects, and keeps his wife and children. A man is able to see beyond himself to the coming generations and knows how his decisions will affect them. He takes responsibility for everyone and everything within his sphere of authority.

All of this is simple, but none of this is easy. The word that Paul uses for character in Romans 5:4 is "*dokime*." The idea is of something that has been tested and whose quality has been proven. When we think of developing character, we often think of the big tests or the big trials. No doubt, in life, those will come. However, what prepares you for those big moments in life is the small, seemingly endless constant barrage of little daily tests over and over again. The decisions you make today determine the type of man you'll be tomorrow. You may have been born a male, but each and every day you have to decide what type of man you want to be. What kind of man do you want to become? Then start living like that man today.

IF…

IF

If you can keep your head when all about you
Are losing theirs and blaming it on you,
If you can trust yourself when all men doubt you,
But make allowance for their doubting too;
If you can wait and not be tired by waiting,
Or being lied about, don't deal in lies,
Or being hated, don't give way to hating,
And yet don't look too good, nor talk too wise:

If you can dream—and not make dreams your master;
If you can think—and not make thoughts your aim;
If you can meet with Triumph and Disaster
And treat those two impostors just the same;
If you can bear to hear the truth you've spoken
Twisted by knaves to make a trap for fools,
Or watch the things you gave your life to, broken,
And stoop and build 'em up with worn-out tools:

If you can make one heap of all your winnings
And risk it on one turn of pitch-and-toss,
And lose, and start again at your beginnings
And never breathe a word about your loss;
If you can force your heart and nerve and sinew

To serve your turn long after they are gone,
And so hold on when there is nothing in you
Except the Will which says to them: 'Hold on!'

If you can talk with crowds and keep your virtue,
Or walk with Kings—nor lose the common touch,
If neither foes nor loving friends can hurt you,
If all men count with you, but none too much;
If you can fill the unforgiving minute
With sixty seconds' worth of distance run,
Yours is the Earth and everything that's in it,
And—which is more—you'll be a Man, my son!

Rudyard Kipling

Growing up as a fatherless bastard, I always longed for a male presence in my life to show me the way. Not only a protector and provider, but also a father to give loving but focused direction to my life. I am sure every man feels a bit rudderless and without direction at times, but I think it's fair to say that this general experience gets a dose of testosterone when you are fatherless. Unfortunately, I never found that inspiring coach, teacher, or sage to send me on my way.

However, what I did receive was so much better—God's Son! As a young man coming into the church, I was filled with a Pollyanna-ish utopian ideal of what I thought life in the church would be like…yeah, not so much. However, there are a lot of good godly men out there walking in the way of men and setting an example for others to follow and giving directions on the path; they are just not as abundant as one would hope. I say this to tell you to be that guy. Be the coach, be the teacher, be the sage, or just be the brother that wants to sharpen and be sharpened by other men that God has put in your life. Seek out such men. If that is in print, fantastic! If that is in person, even better!

Rudyard Kipling's, "If" was one of those "print" blessings in my life. The first time I read it, I was so encouraged and inspired that it almost brought tears to my eyes. I said almost! Of all the poems included in this *DudeVotional,* this one is my favorite. I return to it constantly throughout the year, and I am always encouraged by it. You can find cool narrations of it on YouTube as well, which are always fun to listen to. Sometimes when I am in the car or on the treadmill, I'll just listen to it over and over again. Kipling does a masterful job of laying out with proverbial simplicity and balance what a man should aspire to be like.

The closing line of the poem summarizes it well: "Yours is the Earth and everything that's in it, / And—which is more—you'll be a Man, my son!" This is optimistic, directional, and even more importantly than that, fatherly—"you'll be a Man, my son!" The importance of this masculine affirmation and place in the tribe among men cannot be understated. To be a man is something that you must strive for.

In this respect, being a man is not only a noun but also a verb. Becoming a man is not something that can be accomplished in a classroom. Despite what all of the intelligentsia have told us, this is something that must be passed down by men to men. A generation of men raised by women lack this. However, if they take to heart the words of this poem, I believe it will not only resonate with but also awaken something primitive in their masculine soul.

Perhaps the most masculine thing about "If" is the word "*if*." Sure, Kipling describes manly virtues better than anyone, but the entire poem is conditional. Becoming a man is something that is learned, trained, and honed through action. It is almost as if Kipling thought through the whole gauntlet of manly experiences and thought, "How would a man respond?" and then concluded, "Go and do that! Go and be that kind of man!"

What kind of man? A stable one. Be the kind of man that can keep his head about him when everyone else is losing theirs. Think of all of the panic porn and hysteria that went on during all of the Covid crazy. The most sensible voices were also the most stable. How were those people treated? They were silenced and blamed for everything. However, those who were not deterred and remained stable and consistent not only look like geniuses now, but they also acquired something that the opposition tried to acquire by force but couldn't achieve—namely, respect and authority. One image I like to think of when I consider stability as a man is Stonewall Jackson sitting upright on his horse unmoved and undeterred while bullets fly by. An awesome nickname like that is something you have to earn, and he did. I want to be that kind of man.

What kind of man? A man of resolute confidence. Confidence shouldn't be confused with brash, bombastic bravado. Confidence is earned through knowing yourself and what you are capable of. This doesn't need to be telegraphed to the world; it just needs to be done. Confidence says, "I can, and I will." I will get it done regardless of shortcomings or obstacles. I will get it done. I know that men doubt me, and I understand that, but I don't really care. I will prove them wrong, and I will get it done.

Confidence is the result of consistency and hard work, over and over again. You put in the work, you put in the time, you make the sacrifices, and it doesn't much matter what people say—put your head down and get it done.

What kind of man? A man who is patient, resilient, and humble. Ironically, just waiting is hard work and can often times be exhausting. Patience is a fruit of the Spirit and is something every man should pray for. Patience is not laziness nor an excuse not to act; it is simply knowing when and where and how to act. Also, if you are seeking to grow into a godly man, you will face opposition.

Others will lie about you and hate you. Why? Because they will see what you are becoming, and it will remind them of what they are not. Don't respond in kind, you will be just like them. However, don't think too much of yourself in that you are not like them, and remember that it is only by the grace of God that you are not. Never put on an air of superiority by looking too good and talking too wise. Nobody likes that dude, and you don't either, so don't become him.

What kind of man? A man who can dream but not live in the clouds. A man who can think deeply with the intent of calculated action, not to live in a cocoon of thought. A man who can think well is good, but a man who can think and act is better. A man that can face whatever comes his way—triumph or disaster—and not be swayed by either. A man who knows that whatever he puts out into the world for public consumption will also be subject to ridicule, attack, and manipulation. Don't jump into a pigpen. You'll just get dirty, and pigs will always be pigs. Also, a man knows that failure is not final nor fatal. Everybody loves a comeback, and God raises the dead.

What kind of man? A man who is not afraid to take risks. When failures and losses come, which they will, he is able to get back at it and not complain about it. Are you still breathing? Good, dust yourself off and get back in the game. What did you learn? You just got a world-class education from the school of hard knocks, and the good news is it was still cheaper than college, and the knowledge you acquired is more useful. A man who can be completely exhausted, empty, and broken and be at the end of his tether and still not quit. A man who knows that sometimes simply holding on is a victory.

What kind of man? A man who can achieve fame but not be impressed nor changed by it. A man who can talk to kings and commoners alike and treat them all the same. A man who listens to others but is not a people pleaser. A man who knows that life is short and sucks the marrow out of every minute. A man who is disciplined and productive and prioritizes his time accordingly is worthy of respect.

If you can strive after all of these things and aspire to be that type of man, yours is the earth and everything that is in it, and—which is more—you'll be a man, my son! Masculinity is a long, arduous climb up a steep and rocky hill, and those who keep climbing regardless of the cuts and bruises along the way are rewarded with the most magnificent views. However, every step along the way is prefaced with the word "*if*." Will you do these things? Will you become this kind of man, so much so that men will call you a man? It is really up to you—masculinity begins and is developed by you taking responsibility for your actions and putting one foot in front of the other.

SHEPHERD

I Was a Wondering Sheep

I was a wandering sheep,
I did not love the fold;
I did not love my Shepherd's voice,
I would not be controlled.
I was a wayward child,
I did not love my home;
I did not love my Father's voice,
I loved afar to roam.

The Shepherd sought His sheep,
The Father sought His child;
They followed me o'er vale and hill,
O'er deserts waste and wild;
They found me nigh to death,
Famished and faint and lone;
They bound me with the bands of love,
They saved the wand'ring one.

They spoke in tender love,
They raised my drooping head,
They gently closed my bleeding wounds,
My fainting soul they fed;
They washed my filth away,
They made me clean and fair;
They brought me to my home in peace,
The long sought wanderer.

Jesus my Shepherd is:
'Twas He that loved my soul;
'Twas He that washed me in His blood,
'Twas He that made me whole.
'Twas He that sought the lost,
That found the wand'ring sheep,
'Twas He that brought me to the fold,
'Tis He that still doth keep.

No more a wandering sheep,
I love to be controlled;
I love my tender Shepherd's voice,
I love the peaceful fold.
No more a wayward child,
I seek no more to roam;
I love my heavenly Fathers voice,
I love, I love His home!

Horatius Bonar

I heard a quote the other day, and it was one of those masculine quotes that as soon as you hear it, it just sounds tough and cool. However, this time, as soon as I heard it, I instantaneously and audibly resounded. The quote was this: "In order to catch a wolf, you can't be a sheep. In order to catch a wolf, you have to be a wolf." Now it's true, wolves hunt sheep, and there really isn't anything that sheep can do about it.

They really have no natural line of defense against a wolf. The analogy is easy to spot. This world is filled with evil, wicked people. It is filled with wolves that will hunt and devour, and evil never stops itself. Being sheepish in the face of evil isn't going to "win" them over despite what many evangellyfish may want to believe. I wish this was the case. I wish we could win everyone over with kindness, or as the old saying goes, "kill them with kindness." Unfortunately, wishing will not make it so.

So then, what do you do? Evil people we will always have among us. Is the only way to defend against them to be like them? Is it really true that you have to become a wolf to catch a wolf? If this is the case, where does it end? Wouldn't you then need a wolf to take you out? Everyone who hears that thinks, "No, because when I am a wolf, I will be the good kind of wolf," but that's not how it works.

Anyway, like I said, it sounds cool on the surface but creates just as many problems as it solves. So then, how do you protect the sheep against the wolves? Well, you don't need a wolf to catch a wolf; you need a shepherd. Most men hear that and think that doesn't sound very tough, in part, because our minds have been shaped by a misrepresentation of what shepherds were like in the ancient Near East.

Everyone loves shepherds; they're a staple in every nativity scene and every children's Christmas play. Shepherds have become the perfect prop. All the leftover kids that don't have a part in the play, you can just dress them up like a shepherd (throw a robe on them and put a stick in their hand and you're good) and throw them in the back corner of the stage, and it's the perfect photo op. All this to say that when we think of shepherds, we have nice sentimental feelings because we think of Linus from Charlie Brown and every kid that has been dressed as a shepherd at some point in their life if they grew up in the church. Because of this, we just think shepherds must be cute, like everything else surrounding Christmas, right?

Or we've been conditioned by all of the art with a clean-cut shepherd with long flowing locks of hair delicately holding a baby sheep in his arms with the 23rd Psalm written somewhere in the background. However, this modern cultural picture that has been so ingrained in our psyche couldn't be further from the truth.

By the time of Jesus' birth, shepherds were not so widely loved and adored. They were considered to be gruff and uneducated, and because they had to watch their flocks seven days a week, they were also considered ceremonially unclean and were treated as such. And because their flocks didn't understand property lines, they often had to trespass on other people's property, earning them the reputation of often confusing mine and thine. Needless to say, being a shepherd was not a widely respected profession, nor did anyone think shepherds were cute, and certainly nobody dressed their kids up like them.

If you want a modern-day equivalent, think of roofers. Being a roofer is a very difficult, physically exhausting, dangerous, and thankless job. Because of this, roofers are generally a pretty gruff group. If you wanted your children's Christmas play to be more accurate, you'd tell little Billy to take his shirt off and give him a cigarette and Red Bull. This would be the most spectacular Christmas play ever.

Not to mention that shepherds had two pieces of equipment that were necessary to perform their job. That is, the rod and the staff. The staff was a long stick with a hook at the end of it. This was used primarily for guiding and directing the sheep. The rod was a short, heavy club that was used to beat the snot out of predators. When your only defensive weapon against a multitude of predators (like wolves and even lions) is a short club, you've got to be a pretty tough dude in order to survive.

Shepherds were a gruff lot, however; it was because their vocation demanded it. They needed to be tough and even dangerous when necessary. This was all for the sake of the safety of the sheep, which they were willing to lay their lives down for even though sheep can be remarkably stupid and have an uncanny ability to wander where they ought not. Also, they were there to guide and direct the sheep to keep them out of harm's way. We should be able to see that their toughness and gruffness were rooted in compassion.

This is all necessary backdrop for a couple of reasons. First, and secondarily, "shepherd" was the preferred term for leadership in the early church and is a term we still use to this day, even though the vocation is uncommon to most of us. However, it is very important for us to understand that when this term was used, they were not thinking of Linus or how cute your kid looks in an oversized robe in the background of the church Christmas play. They were thinking of men who existed on the border of civilization and the wilderness, men who were every bit as tough and dangerous as they were tender. Men who loved their sheep and had a job to do regardless of what the intelligentsia may have said about them.

Second, and primarily, this helps us to understand how Christ, our great King, cares for and protects us as the great Shepherd and Overseer of our souls. This should also humble us in that we were all at one point wandering sheep, who did not love the fold. We did not love the Good Shepherd's voice, nor would we be controlled. We are, as the old hymn says, "Prone to wander, Lord, I feel it, prone to leave the God I love."

Yet our Good Shepherd leaves the 99 to come for us in the cold, dark, black of night. With His rod and His staff, He pursues us with an unperturbed pace. "The Shepherd sought His sheep, / The Father sought His child. / They followed me o'er vale and hill, / O'er deserts waste and wild; / They found me nigh to death, / Famished and faint and lone; / They bound me with the bands of love, / They saved the wand'ring one." (lines 9-16).

Jesus, the Good Shepherd, will lose none of His sheep. He will find and rescue every last one. No matter how dark, no matter how far, no matter how broken, hurt, confused, ashamed, guilty, or lonely. Jesus died for every last one that the Father has given Him, and He will lose none. He will find them. He will save them. He binds and heals what is broken. He will forgive the guilty and cleanse the defiled. He will rescue the lost and bring them home, and He will bring the dead to life. He is not only the standard of what a shepherd is; He is the standard of what a man is to be. "Jesus sought me when a stranger, / Wandering from the fold of God; / He, to rescue me from danger, / Interposed His precious blood." ("Come, Thou Fount of Every Blessing," lines 13-16).

He interposed for us. He didn't just stand in between you and everything that would seek to ravage and devour you. He took all that your sin deserved upon Himself. He conquered Satan and sin and through His resurrection, and with His righteous rod, He beat death itself. Through the blood of Jesus, death no longer has any sting for you or hold over you.

We were wandering sheep. Think of the toughness and tenderness that it took to save you. The picture we should have of Jesus, which is certainly more accurate than the effeminate, soft, flowing-hair Jesus, is that of a blood-covered shepherd as he beats to death a pack of wolves that are seeking to devour one of His lost sheep. Jesus my Shepherd is: 'Twas He that loved my soul…how? 'Twas He that washed me in His blood…how? 'Twas He that made me whole…how? 'Twas He that sought the lost, that found the wand'ring sheep…how? 'Twas He that brought me to the fold…how? 'Tis He that still doth keep…how?

The minute you answer the how to all of the actions of Jesus, you not only realize how deeply personal your salvation is and the cost that was paid, but it also enables you to see the rugged toughness and tenderness of our Great Shepherd in a whole new way. Jesus is our Good Shepherd. He pursued us, He saved us, He cleansed us, He protects us, He provides for us, He leads and guides us, He defends us, He corrects us, and so on.

In Christ, as men, we are under shepherds of those whom Christ has entrusted to our care. We represent what Christ is like to those whom we are responsible for. Do they see Christ in you? Are you tough and tender at the right time, in the right way, and with the right people? The only way to shepherd like the Good Shepherd is to know the Good Shepherd well and know what He has done, is doing, and will do for you. Love Him, seek Him, obey Him, pray to Him constantly, and do everything in your power to be like Him. Be tough and be tender. Be dangerous and be gentle. Be a shepherd like our Good Shepherd.

FIGHT

Do Not Go Gentle into That Good Night

Do not go gentle into that good night,
Old age should burn and rave at close of day;
Rage, rage against the dying of the light.

Though wise men at their end know dark is right,
Because their words had forked no lightning they
Do not go gentle into that good night.

Good men, the last wave by, crying how bright
Their frail deeds might have danced in a green bay,
Rage, rage against the dying of the light.

Wild men who caught and sang the sun in flight,
And learn, too late, they grieved it on its way,
Do not go gentle into that good night.

Grave men, near death, who see with blinding
sight
Blind eyes could blaze like meteors and be gay,
Rage, rage against the dying of the light.

And you, my father, there on the sad height,
Curse, bless, me now with your fierce tears, I pray.
Do not go gentle into that good night.
Rage, rage against the dying of the light.

Dylan Thomas

In many respects all of life is one big fat scrap, one big fat fight. From the very first breath to the very last, we are engaged in some type of battle, or so it would seem. No growth comes without pain, and unfortunately growth and change are signs of life. Therefore, if we want to live, we have no choice but to gird up our loins and get after it. We have to face the storm head-on and walk into the fray, into the hurricane of life, come what may.

Men were designed for this. We were created to rule and have dominion over the earth. We were charged to guard and keep the Garden, and though sin has entered the world, we are still charged to guard and keep all that the Almighty has entrusted to our care. Every man is going to have battles to face in his life. This takes different shapes for different men, but we will all have things in our lives to overcome.

We see this early on in boys. I have two sons and three daughters, and I can tell you what every parent since the beginning of time has discovered and what you already know: boys and girls are different. My daughters wanted to nurture and hold every baby doll they ever saw, while my sons saw all of those same dolls as potential enemy combatants. Also, I do not think there is a material or substance on earth that they couldn't turn into a weapon or a tool in some capacity. My point being, they are wired for dominion, and they intuitively know that, at some point, that will require them to do battle.

There is obviously a context here that should determine and direct the conditions of engagement. Erring off of the road to the right is just as bad as erring off the road to the left, and you can't course correct one ditch by jumping into the other. The soft, effeminate passivist is obviously erring off the road to the left. This is not to say that a man needs to be jacked or part of special forces. This is more of a masculine disposition and a willingness to do one's duty as a man. That is, you could be a soft-spoken, physically weaker guy, but when the time comes, you are willing to stand up for those weaker than yourself or are willing to sacrifice yourself for the sake of women and children being threatened. A man that endures physical harm because he interposed for women and children or those weaker than himself is an honorable man. Regardless of his frame, he has a masculine disposition and is willing to play the man.

The opposite of this is also true. The hard, strong, aggressive guy may be erring off the road to the right, though not necessarily so. However, guys can use this as an excuse to be a cantankerous prick. This is the guy that is just insufferable to be around because everything is a battle and everyone is an enemy combatant, and they don't know where and when and how to pick their battles, so they end up fighting with everyone. In many respects these guys are guilty of the same sin as the wet-noodle femmie guy. That is, men are wired to guard and keep—it's in the bones. The problem is the only thing they are ultimately guarding and keeping is themselves. They are ultimately motivated by fear and not love for others. So then, these guys may look the part, but they are not honorable.

Jordan Peterson said, "A harmless man is not a good man. A good man is a very, very dangerous man who has that under voluntary control." I believe this resonates with men because it is in their bones as men. The goal would be to be a dangerous man that is so God-directed, self-controlled, and self-disciplined that when you exercise your masculine capacities for guarding and keeping, God is pleased and those under your care are protected, loved, and built up. This would mean that you are not causing them harm, nor allowing them to be harmed. Remove the threats without becoming one yourself. This is the ultimate masculine battle that you fight within.

Every man understands that there are obstacles, trials, temptations, and opposition to overcome in this life. Every man also understands that these battles are not only without but within. The toughest opponent every man has to conquer every day of his life is the one that is staring back at him in the mirror every morning. The way to keep oneself from erring to the right or to the left is to win these daily battles with self as you war against Satan, sin, and the flesh. Of course these battles are won when fought with an alien righteousness, an alien strength. That is, a strength and a righteousness that is not our own but that comes through faith in Jesus Christ.

However, despite all of our great differences as men—families, backgrounds, experiences, cultures, economics, sufferings, hardships, and on and on and on—we all have one thing in common, one battle we must all fight. It is always there; it's always in the backdrop of our lives, so much so that the lifelong fear of it motivates most of our decisions, though most of the time subconsciously. Death chases us around all of our lives and is always there, always tapping at the chamber door like Poe's raven.

We can ignore it, we can deny it, we can run from it, and we can even try to fight it, but there it is. As soon as we enter into this world and take our first breath, we have an expiration date we know not when. Rage, rage against the dying of the light, but that last breath will come, and we will die. Though all of the unknowns surrounding death are terrifying, what scares us most is that it is appointed for all men to die once, and then comes judgment. We will all stand before the Almighty and His judgment seat and give an account of the deeds done in the flesh.

Death is coming for us all, and there is absolutely nothing we can do about it. However, before this day comes like a thief in the night, our bodies begin eroding and degenerating until everything just eventually fails. Anyone reading this who has been alive long enough knows that aging is a sport of attrition that no one ultimately wins. Aging is the slow descent to death and a letting go of everything you once loved and most likely took for granted.

Is aging difficult? Absolutely, aging can be a merciless bitch. There is nothing easy about it. However, when done well, there is a certain beauty and strength in it. When it doesn't break you, it creates a resiliency that has its own beauty and strength that goes along with it. A woman in her

60s does not have the same youthful beauty that she did in her 20s but this doesn't mean she doesn't have beauty. There is a certain beauty that can come with age. Likewise, a man in his 60s does not have the strength that he did in his 20s, but this doesn't mean that he doesn't have a different kind of strength.

Those who age well know they are getting closer to glory; in fact, that is what enables them to age well. Therefore, though hard, there is a certain radiance there. The inverse of this is also true. Because they are chasing something that is impossible to obtain, like trying to catch the wind, they grow hard and more cynical. Instead of becoming more real and more substantial, trying to hold onto a fading glory that was meant to remain under the sun, they actually become less real—they become plastic. In some cases, literally.

One of the many ironies and paradoxes of life is that the way you face and fight against death determines the quality of your life. One approach is the Ned Flanders, okily-dokily type of Christian who pretends that death will be fun because Jesus conquered the grave. Therefore there is no reason to fight against death at all. We should actually skip towards it while whistling a happy tune.

Another approach is not necessarily to deny it, but just to pretend like you're not going there, which is evident by the fact that you are not aging at all—or so you want people to believe. This is the guy on TRT with the porcelain grill that looks like horse teeth who uses Just for Men and gets plastic surgery. Despite what this guy may believe, he isn't fooling anyone, especially his organs and joints.

Yet another approach is to look death in the face with a stoic, steely resolve like Maximus from Gladiator and say, "Death smiles at us all; all we can do is smile back." Obviously this is not exhaustive. We know the crotchety old prick who seems to surpass himself and progress in crotchetiness with each passing year in part because he is in perpetual pain and in part because he is terrified. Or the shut-in who has just quit life and is clock-watching, waiting to die. But, for the most part, I am assuming most reading this are going to fall into one of the above three general categories, for which there is a nugget of truth in each.

The okily-dokily guy is wrong in removing the weightiness of death, almost making it trite. The wages for sin is death, and we should mourn over it. However, Christ did conquer the grave, and it is nothing that we should fear, knowing that in Christ, death has lost its sting. Yes, we will all die, and then comes judgment, but Christ, our wrath-bearing substitute, received our judgment. He died our death, He drank up the full cup of God's wrath, and through repentance and faith in Him, we are given new life. However, in order to experience the full joy and pleasures of that new life, we must die, and until we get to that point, we experience a slow death and must continually let go of things that we may be holding ever so tightly too.

The jacked 60-year-old with horse teeth is right to want to hold on to life as long as he can; however, he is missing the mark, prolonging the inevitable, and actually robbing himself of a strength that is gained only through suffering. As a man, it is easy to understand that one would want to hold on to their strength and vitality as long as they can. However, no matter how impressive of a physical specimen you may be, you are going to have to let go of some of that as you age.

No matter who you are, things are going to get progressively harder and more painful. Can you embrace all of that and keep moving forward? The more and more we lose ourselves, the more we find ourselves, but this only happens when we embrace the greater purpose for which we were created, namely the glory of God. With that in mind, trying to fool others (maybe even ourselves) that we are not getting closer and closer to death seems more than just a little silly.

Counter to this approach, Maximus was right. Death is coming for us all, and denying that or trying to convince others otherwise is not wise. Also, the ideal of living honorably until that day comes and then desiring to die honorably when that day comes is a noble desire. However, said nobility is going to hit a brick wall and be in for a very rude awakening if death comes outside of Christ and one is bearing the weight of their sin before the judgment seat of God. Aware of this, it would seem as though a little more ragging and a little less smiling would be reasonable.

So then, how do we fight this battle? Well, first, it's okay to want to hold onto your strength and vitality as long as you can. Bodily training is good for much, but it is not the end. Eventually, we will have to let go of everything. Does this suck? Yes and no. God is a gracious and good God. Through the loss, through the letting go and grinding through it, we gain grit, we gain gratitude in the Lord, we gain wisdom, we gain maturity, and so on. Character does not grow in the soil of ease. God teaches much and shows us much of Himself as we get closer and closer to death. The irony is, the more you try to hold on to life, the more you lose it, becoming more brittle in the process.

Also, in Christ, we should be able to smile at death, not in a stupid okily-dokily type of way that not only trivializes death but also life. However, we don't smile at death with a cool, calm indifference, come what may. We smile at death with a weighty joy and optimism, knowing full well that our great King has conquered the grave. Death will come for us, but it will not be our end. The apostle Paul said, "To live is Christ and to die is gain." (Phil.1:21). Paul too looked death in the face and smiled at it, not necessarily because he was smiling at death, but because he was smiling at the One who conquered it. Death is a shadow, and Paul could see the light of Christ through it.

So then, how do we fight this battle? How do we not go gentle into the good night and rage against the light? We do so with a weighty, yet maybe even a plucky optimism, asking the Lord to teach us to number our days alright so that through the wisdom of Christ we will be prepared for a time when days will no longer need to be numbered.

Fight

LEGACY

Ozymandias

I met a traveller from an antique land,
Who said—"Two vast and trunkless legs of stone
Stand in the desert. . . . Near them, on the sand,
Half sunk a shattered visage lies, whose frown,
And wrinkled lip, and sneer of cold command,
Tell that its sculptor well those passions read
Which yet survive, stamped on these lifeless things,
The hand that mocked them, and the heart that fed;
And on the pedestal, these words appear:
My name is Ozymandias, King of Kings;
Look on my Works, ye Mighty, and despair!
Nothing beside remains. Round the decay
Of that colossal Wreck, boundless and bare
The lone and level sands stretch far away."

Percy Bysshe Shelley

How do you want to be remembered when you die? Tough question, I know. Here is a tougher one; well, at least it is more challenging and humbling to ask: if you were to die today, how would people remember you? That one hurts a little bit more, because it forces you to at least be a little more honest with yourself. That is, if you honestly evaluate where you are currently at in every area of your life.

Unfortunately, we all have an uncanny ability to grade ourselves on a curve. And, if in the rare case we are actually honest with ourselves and we come to the very reasonable conclusion that we could be doing better with our lives, well then, we just find a pool of poor schmucks doing worse, and then we are justified by association. Yes, we say, "I could be doing better than I am, but I am definitely doing better than this guy." However, when you make fools the standard by which you judge yourself, you can pretty much guarantee that you will be counted among them.

Our self-delusion seems to be even more impressive when applied to the future. We all remember when we were kids and we wanted to be this, that, or the other. Most of us knew, even as children, that this was just idle chatter and was really nothing more than wishful thinking not taking into account abilities, aptitudes, desires, and even the laws of logic and physics in many cases. Despite this, kids should dream big and have a wonderful and stupendous running storyboard in their mind of everything they can be and do with the life that God has given them.

However, somewhere along the line we get so busy living that we fail to take into account what kind of life we're living. This reminds me of a line from the movie *Ferris Bueller's Day Off*, "Life moves pretty fast. If you don't stop and look around once in a while, you could miss it." It is very easy for us to get caught up in what's commonly known as the *rat race,* so that we don't know what we're living for or what we are willing to die for. As a result, most men haven't really given very serious thought to the question, "How do you want to be remembered when you die?" That day seems far away, and they are just trying to get through the week ahead.

If one were to be asked this question point-blank, I am sure many would come up with some meaningful answers that are truly substantive and not completely superficial. At this point, regardless of whatever answers are given, the obvious and painful follow-up question would be, what are you doing today to achieve that end?

Again, because we are so busy, ever so busy, and because death always seems far away, we haven't slowed down enough to think about such things. Unfortunately, the merciless hands of time never stop turning, and life really does fly by. Minutes turn into hours that turn into days that turn into months that turn into years that turn into decades, and that's only if you are given a good long life—which is not a given!

What you do with your time on a regular basis adds up to the sum total of your life, and life can't be lived backwards. Sooner or later we will all sit down at a banquet of consequences—some to feast and some to famine. Sitting down at the table is not the time to sow seed. Psalm 90:12 states, "So teach us to number our days that we may get a heart of wisdom."

It seems that there is a growing sentiment among men to push back against the spirit of our age. This is seen in the rejection of the toxic feminism that has been violently shoved down our throats for decades, but this is also seen in that more and more men want their lives to count for something. This is good, in that men were made for dominion, to build, create, expand, cultivate, and conquer. But here again, we are daily sowing seeds that will someday determine what type of harvest we will reap.

Herein lies much of the weakness with a particular type of grind culture that is popular among men who don't sit down to pee. It is natural and good that men want to push themselves to be better and to strive for more. This is not just a rejection of the zeitgeist of our age but also of much of evangelicalism that has created and perpetuated soft and mediocre men under the guise of piety.

However, before one sets out for greatness, it is genuinely a good idea to know what target you're shooting at. Where you are aiming is most likely what you're going to hit. I have been telling women for over a decade in ministry they can't have it all. At least not the "all" as defined by feminism. There is simply no way to be the super-impressive boss-bitch who is working 50+ hours a week while at the same time being supermom. No matter how awesome, competent, and skilled you may be, you can't have it all. Sure, some people are better at managing their time than others, but at the end of the day we are all still only left with 24 hours in the day.

The same is true for men. No matter how awesome we are and no matter how badly we may want to buck every trend and prove that we alone are the exception to the rule, we are not. We are not God; we are not omnipresent. Some may be better at managing their time than others; in some cases, much better. However they are still working with the same amount of time as everyone else. And to top it all off, we all have an expiration date. As humbling as that may be, when that day comes, the sum total of your days will determine how you'll be remembered.

This presents us with the concept of opportunity cost. If you spend your time on A, you can't, at the same time and in the same way, spend your time on B. The cost of A, therefore, is B. The opportunity cost is what is given up in order to have something else. There is simply no way around this one. No matter how much time, money, or talent you may have, you can't have it all; you're not God.

Setting goals is a good thing, and working hard to accomplish them is a good thing. It is also important to point out that the habits that are developed to get from A to B, and the character that is created and cultivated through the process, are of even more value than the accomplishment of said goal. All of this is of great value, but what is given up getting from A to B might not be. Herein lie some of the problems with grind culture, that is, prioritization and opportunity cost.

Many men who have accomplished much and are inspirational in their own right will even say this much: you can't be balanced and great. They will say that you have to be all in and obsessed. Perhaps this is what is necessary in accomplishing a goal, but this says nothing about what is given up in order to accomplish said goal. Running ultramarathons, lifting massive amounts of weight, achieving career milestones, and starting and building a company are awesome things in and of themselves, but we don't exist on an island. Being driven and focused is a good thing if what you are focused on and driving towards is good.

Let's just say that you accomplish everything you set out to accomplish in life, so much so that people look at you and think, "Wow, you really are amazing." However, your wife and kids think that you are a selfish prick because you spent all of your time developing yourself and accomplishing your goals. Again, self-improvement and goal accomplishments are good, but not if the most important relationships in your life suffer and languish as a result, which, by the way, will determine how you are actually remembered.

So you've run all the miles, lifted all the weights, built all the businesses, and made all the money, and you think you've done something special and created a legacy that will endure. None of those will last, and the only thing you've really built is an empire of dirt right next to Ozymandias that spans across the lone and level sands. Every single last one of your accomplishments will be accomplished, and then some, by someone who comes after you.

If this is all you've given your life to, when you sit down to dine, your plate will be filled with dirt, and your legacy will be bitterness and resentment that will last long beyond you in your children's children's children.

The Lord, through the Apostle Paul, strikes a divine balance for us when he writes, "If you put these things before the brothers, you will be a good servant of Christ Jesus, being trained in the words of the faith and of the good doctrine that you have followed. Have nothing to do with irreverent, silly myths. Rather train yourself for godliness; for while bodily training is of some value, godliness is of value in every way, as it holds promise for the present life and also for the life to come." (1 Timothy 4:6-8).

Bodily training is good; however, godliness is of greater value, as it holds promise for the present life and also for the life to come. The lesson is clear: prioritize your life accordingly. Bodily training is good; however, the earth and everything in it is passing away, including you. The real legacy we leave behind and the real value we add will be seen in the relationships that are closest to us, beginning with the Lord and the pursuit of godliness. This better equips you to pour into your wife and children first and prioritize your time accordingly.

It also should be noted that this is not at the expense of everything else but rather enables you to put it in its proper place. Again, bodily training is good for much, and so too is building a business, running for office, and so on. All of this can be pleasing to the Lord when pursued through the

Lord. Mediocrity and laziness have no place in the church.

In the Parable of the Talents, the only servant who not only did not hear "well done" but rather was cursed and cast out was the one afraid to use and multiply his master's resources. It is terrifying to try to build your kingdom while neglecting those whom the Lord has given you to shepherd. You may hear "well done," but it won't be from God. You may build a kingdom, but in the end it will be an empire of dirt.

You Become Like What You Behold

Life's Mirror

There are loyal hearts, there are spirits brave,
There are souls that are pure and true;
Then give to the world the best that you have,
And the best will come back to you.

Give love, and love to your life will flow,
A strength in your utmost need;
Have faith, and a score of hearts will show
Their faith in your work and deed.

Give truth, and your gift will be paid in kind,
And honor will honor meet;
And the smile which is sweet will surely find
A smile that is just as sweet.

Give sorrow and pity to those who mourn;
You will gather in flowers again
The scattered seeds from your thought outborne
Though the sowing seemed but vain.

For life is the mirror of king and slave,
'Tis just what we are and do;
Then give to the world the best that you have
And the best will come back to you.

Madeline S. Bridges

Man was made in the image and likeness of God. Man is the only copy creature in all of creation. It is almost as if man was created as a living organic mirror, in that we are reflective. That is, whatever we set our hearts towards and our gaze upon, we will not only gravitate towards but also become like. So then, man was created in relationship with God. He was designed to gaze upon Him in all His majesty. He was to walk with Him, behold Him, hear, reflect, and meditate upon His word day and night. As the knowledge of the glory of God filled him, man would then fill all of creation with God's derivative, reflective glory.

To use a paternal example, in many respects we are to be like children pretending to be like our father. Not that we ever mature into gods, but we can grow in maturity, and the closer we get to God, the brighter our reflective glory becomes, and the more He will be seen in us as a result. All this to say that as image bearers of God, we were designed to become like what we behold.

My wife and I have five awesome children, two of whom are currently driving. While teaching them to drive, at some point I told them to be very careful in taking their eyes off of the road. This warning is twofold. First, things happen very quickly, and threats seemingly come out of nowhere, and this usually happens when you are most comfortable and least suspecting. Therefore, in order to mitigate the risks and get to your destination, you have to focus on the road ahead.

Second, we naturally gravitate towards what our eyes are set upon. If you see something unfamiliar, unknown, beautiful, intriguing, or whatever off in the distance that is not directly in front of you, whether it be to the right or the left, you will begin to lean towards that thing. Your hand on the wheel will lean towards what your eyes are set upon. This is why we are warned, "Do not swerve to the right or to the left; turn your foot away from evil." (Prov. 4:27).

So then, given that this is the case, you would think that we would just be in a state of magisterial bliss, being transformed from one degree of glory to the next. Is this what we see under the sun? Yes and no! No, in that man sinned against God. In doing so, he essentially turned his back on God, seeking his glory above the Lord of glory, which sounds remarkably stupid because it is—sin is stupid.

Fallen man is like a mirror gazing upon itself, never getting above, or beyond, or away from itself. Or if you will, natural, fallen man is like a man gazing upon his own reflection in a pond. He is so captivated by his own grandeur that he continually gets closer and closer until he is submerged in water and drowns himself.

Turning your back on the Author of Life will ultimately result in disorder, decay, disunity, and death. However, though fallen, man is still capable of great things because he bears the image of the Almighty. However, despite all of fallen man's greatness that shines through from time to time, he is still only reflecting a shadow. Despite all of his greatness and accomplishments they are all transient and lack weight and substance. A shadow only serves as evidence that true substance and light actually exist.

Our lives are mirrors, but what will those mirrors reflect? Well, they can only reflect what our eyes are set upon. Again, we naturally gravitate towards what our eyes are set upon, and we become like what we behold. What we then behold in our lives should be reflective of what we are and what we do. As Madeline S. Bridges stated above, "For life is the mirror of king and slave, / 'Tis just what we are and do; / Then give to the world the best that you have / and the best will come back to you."

Perhaps we could tweak her words a wee bit by saying that life is a mirror of King and slave, or even that life is a mirror of slave and slave. This means that man will either reflect the Almighty, the King of glory, or that he will reflect his own image, which is a testimony to his bondage and slavery to sin. I believe it was Martin Luther that said man is a beast ridden by one of two masters, either by Christ or the devil.

What this means is that natural man, apart from Christ, is hellbent on following his own will for his own glory, consumed with his own reflection. However, for those for whom Jesus Christ is Lord and Master, they have been brought back into fellowship with the Father through Christ. God the Father sent His Son into the world on a divine rescue mission to seek and to save what was lost, to reclaim His wayward and lost children and bring them back into His fold. Jesus died the death that we deserved to die, thus removing the debt that condemned us. He also lived the obedient, righteous life that we could not.

Through repentance and faith in Christ we are redeemed and reconciled to God, brought into fellowship with the Father, and given a new nature that beholds the glory of God in the face of Jesus Christ. Our new nature longs to be in fellowship with God, knowing more of Him and beholding His power and glory. Our new nature longs to hear from Him and put His words into action. What we are determines what we do.

Furthermore, Jesus Christ, the Son of God, didn't just take on flesh to be our Redeemer, Reconciler, and King; He is also our example. In Christ, we see everything that man was to be and do. Jesus is the perfect image of the invisible God. To see Jesus is to see the Father because Jesus and the Father are one (John 10:30).

Philip, struggling to understand all of this, said to Jesus, "Lord, show us the Father, and it is enough for us." Jesus responded, "Have I been with you so long, and you still do not know me, Philip? Whoever has seen me has seen the Father. How can you say, 'Show us the Father'? Do you not believe that I am in the Father and the Father is in me? The words that I say to you I do not speak on my own authority, but the Father who dwells in me does his works. Believe me that I am in the Father and the Father is in me, or else believe on account of the works themselves." (John 14:8-11).

God hasn't just told us what He is like; He has shown us. God hasn't just told us what is required of us; He has shown us. God has fixed everything that is broken in our relationship with Him through Christ. God has removed every barrier to fellowship with Him through Christ. There is one mediator between God and men, and His name is Jesus. Jesus is the standard of everything that we are to be and do as men.

"Then give to the world the best that you have, / And the best will come back to you." These words are true, for the most part—kind of; they just don't go far enough. God is the God of order and not chaos, and the world is designed as such; cause and effect is a real thing. If you act in such and such a way, you should expect such and such a result. If anyone doubts this, they should just read the book of Proverbs. However, this world is badly broken, of which the book of Ecclesiastes and lived experience will attest.

It is generally true that those who are honest, hardworking, and kind will attract those same types of people to them. It is also true that they will inspire such behavior in others. This is good, as far as it goes, but how far does it really go, and why? Another way of asking this is, for what end and who is glorified in the end?

We all know that there are men who are outside of Christ that exhibit patterns of behavior that are commendable, such as discipline, loyalty, strength, and so on. Is that good? Certainly. Should we aspire to exhibit such character? Certainly, but for entirely different reasons and to entirely different ends, culminating in entirely different results.

Again, we were created as image bearers; it is what we are. Therefore we will become like what we are beholding. Our desire is to be like Christ. Paul said, "Be imitators of me, as I am of Christ." (1 Cor. 11:1). Christ is the end for which we strive. So then, if we see certain attributes exercised in others, such as discipline, strength, loyalty, faithfulness, and so on, that we desire to exhibit more of in our own lives, that desire is not driven to be a better man as an end in and of itself. Rather, that desire is driven to be more like the God-man so that more of Christ would be seen in us. His glory is not a fading glory that exists in the shadowlands, but rather is a glory that removes all such shadows.

C.S. Lewis said, "I believe in Christianity as I believe that the Sun has risen not only because I see it but because by it I see everything else." Therefore, when I see discipline in others, I can rejoice because I see more of Christ. When I see faithfulness and self-sacrifice exhibited in others, I can rejoice because I see more of Christ, and in seeing more of Christ, I see more of what I need to aspire to be and do.

Some may hear that and think, what's the difference if the actions are the same? The difference is that the results aren't the same, ultimately speaking. Now, one may argue that discipline, for example, is a reward in and of itself. Certainly, there are benefits to having discipline as opposed to being undisciplined, but apart from Christ, all of your discipline will end up in the grave right along with you.

To quote Bridges again, "Then give to the world the best that you have / And the best will come back to you." If we are of the world, the best we have to give is of the world. If we are only reflecting that which is transient and passing away, then that is all we ultimately have to give. We want to imitate Christ so that we have something of ultimate value and substance to give. In Christ, we desire to give something far beyond ourselves, Christ Himself being the best we have to give.

One may also argue that when we do this, that is, earnestly desire to imitate Christ and live for Christ, the best is often not what we get back; in fact, sometimes it feels like just the opposite. The answer to this is yes, but also not so much. In that, the problem is really one of perspective. We want Proverbs, but we are living Ecclesiastes. This is because the world is broken, but take heart, in Christ we are not of this world. In Christ, we transcend it. The best that is coming back to us in Christ, far surpasses anything this world has to offer, at least in its current state.

Therefore, when we read "Life's Mirror," we can give it an Amen because we see loyalty, bravery, purity of heart, love, strength, faithfulness, truthfulness, kindness, honor, and so on as actions that are pleasing to God through Christ. Not only that, but we also see all such behavior as preparatory for a life beyond this life, where the best is truly yet to come. However, this best that is yet to come is not the consequence of our life, but rather of Christ's.

Your Excuses Are Lies

It Couldn't Be Done

Somebody said that it couldn't be done
    But he with a chuckle replied
That "maybe it couldn't," but he would be one
    Who wouldn't say so till he'd tried.
So he buckled right in with the trace of a grin
    On his face. If he worried he hid it.
He started to sing as he tackled the thing
    That couldn't be done, and he did it!

Somebody scoffed: "Oh, you'll never do that;
    At least no one ever has done it;"
But he took off his coat and he took off his hat
    And the first thing we knew he'd begun it.
With a lift of his chin and a bit of a grin,
    Without any doubting or quiddit,
He started to sing as he tackled the thing
    That couldn't be done, and he did it.

There are thousands to tell you it cannot be done,
    There are thousands to prophesy failure,
There are thousands to point out to you one by one,
    The dangers that wait to assail you.
But just buckle in with a bit of a grin,
    Just take off your coat and go to it;
Just start in to sing as you tackle the thing
    That "cannot be done," and you'll do it.

Edgar Albert Guest

As soon as I heard it, I thought, "That's awesome," and "One day, I am totally going to use that for something in some way." Well, dear friends, today is that day. We can all thank Jocko Willink for the title for the chapter. Someone wrote to Jocko's podcast seeking his advice regarding their seemingly endless ability to make excuses in life. They specifically wanted to know how to stop making excuses.

Jocko answered in the following way, "How do you stop making excuses? That is actually pretty simple. And I said it the other day, and you have to realize… You have to know, you have to accept—that all your excuses are lies. They are lies. All of them." He continued, "Think about the things that you tell yourself. The lies you used to used to rationalize, taking the easy road and leaving discipline behind. Think about them. You don't have time? That's a lie. You don't have support? You don't have the equipment or the gear? Lies. You don't know "the best way"? Who cares. That's a lie. Or you're too old, or you're too young—of course you're too old or too young. Lie. And there's the 'you're too busy'… Sure you are. That's a lie. Or you're too tired, too sore, or you're just plain not feeling it… Lies, lies, lies. And the list goes on and on and on. And it doesn't stop if you don't make it stop."

He then went on to say that the way to make the lies stop is with the truth, because the truth will set you free. I wouldn't presume to know the state of Jocko's soul, but that's good stuff. Most people have an uncanny ability to self-sabotage, perpetuated by excuse after excuse after excuse. We all do it and will continue to do so until we've had enough. Most never get beyond that point because they are not ready for the answers to questions that they already know. It is true, the truth does set you free if you are willing to receive it, but before you receive it, it usually hurts real good.

What keeps you from accomplishing your goals? What keeps you from becoming the person you desire to be? What keeps you from eating better? What keeps you from being in better shape? What keeps you from having a better relationship with your wife and children? What keeps you from reading or writing that book or picking up that hobby? What keeps you from all of the things you want to accomplish? What keeps you from becoming a better person? The list goes on and on. Even as you read those words, you probably have your inner defense attorney mounting a case to find you innocent.

However, the one common denominator in all of the above questions is you. It hurts, I know, but there is no way around it; the road to self-improvement begins with you, which means the first dragon you have to slay every morning is the one staring back at you in the mirror. This also means that we have to come to terms with the fact that we are where we are because of decisions that we have made. Again, this hurts, but I think if you're honest with yourself, you would agree. In the words of Teddy Roosevelt, "If you could kick the person in the pants responsible for most of your trouble, you wouldn't sit for a month."

There are those who will read the above and get all huffy-puffy and play the ever-prominent and ever-popular victim. There are true victims that have all kinds of horrible shit that they have to deal with as a result of what has been done to them. I am not denying any of this or trying to minimize one's suffering in any degree, nor am I saying that those who are truly victims are responsible for what has happened to them. Not at all! I've experienced enough in my own life and have heard enough stories throughout ministry that will break you. So I get it.

However, I also know that the way to heal and move on is not to allow yourself to be defined by the stuff that has happened to you. It is hard, and the only way through the whirlwind is to wrestle with God. All the garbage that has happened to you can be a chapter in your story, or it can be the entirety of your story, but again, you have the power to determine that. You may not have been in control of what happened to you, but you are in control of how you respond to it and what you do with your life from here on out. Turn to Christ, give it to Christ, seek the healing that only Christ can provide, be strengthened in Christ, and overcome. Refuse to let other people define your journey, your life, especially those who hurt you. Stop giving them any power over you.

Perhaps one of the saddest things about the glorification of victimhood in our culture is that most decrying victimization are not really victims at all but simply use it as a crutch to hide behind to excuse laziness, mediocrity, and fear. In this respect, victimization is made a virtue signal that the rest of us are for some reason meant to pay for. This is sick and self-aggrandizing and is often driven by envy. This is like the friend of a person who has cancer and sees the support they receive. They then declare that they have cancer as well and demand that you sympathize with them and pay for their healthcare. Do they really have cancer—how dare you ask!

I heard someone say a little while back that the hero and the villain are both alike, defined by their pain. The villain is hurt by others and says, "I am going to make everyone else experience the same pain I have." The hero is also hurt by others or circumstances or whatever and says, "I am going to do everything in my power to protect others from going through the same." The pain is similar, but the response to it couldn't be more different.

Either way, both were in control of the course of their lives. Our culture has become so perverse that we excuse the villain because he is a victim, and we punish the hero for reminding us how bad the rest of us suck. It is a painful realization when you look at others who have experienced so much pain and have no earthly advantages whatsoever to speak of, and yet they are doing better than you and doing it joyfully.

However, outside of legitimate victimhood and the mentally ill made-up kind that is so prevalent today are the people in your life that are just a cancer. These are the people filled with negative energy. They are always there to tell you all the reasons why you can't or won't accomplish this, that, or the other. "Somebody said that it couldn't be done…Somebody scoffed: 'Oh, you'll never do that; / At least no one ever has done it;'…There are thousands to tell you it cannot be done, / There are thousands to prophesy failure, / There are thousands to point out to you one by one, / The dangers that wait to assail you."

Just a couple quick words about these people. One, they suck; however, if you listen to them, you suck. You don't have to give these people an audience, nor are they entitled to any place in your life. The only reason they have an audience with you is because you give them one. If you want to dry out the lawn, kink the hose. Also, the vast majority of the time, not only are these people not happy, they are downright miserable. Why, on God's green earth, are you taking life advice from people who have a life you don't want? These people will keep you from becoming the man you want to be and then secretly rejoice if you fail any particular endeavor because they see it as a validation of their suckery.

Second, we need to heed the advice of Kipling and make allowance for their doubting too. I am in no way minimizing people who suck and stand by the above statements. However, we have to be brutally honest with ourselves so that we understand why people may be saying what they are saying and why they may have doubts. This will make the obstacles more clear and even sweeter when they are overcome. Having a little chip on your shoulder and desiring to prove people wrong isn't necessarily a bad thing and can be a helpful motivator.

Unfortunately, victim culture is just as prevalent in the church as it is in the world, but even outside of that there seems to be a mass acceptance of self-deprecation and avoidance of anything that resembles self-improvement. Some of this is because of theological wack-jobs who preach a gospel of self-centeredness. This is obviously not what I am talking about here, and we are right to have an aversion to those people and their message. However, we should be able to thread the needle here, and there is no need to flush the baby with the bathwater.

The book of Proverbs has a lot of unfavorable things to say about the sluggard and an equal and opposite amount of favorable things to say about hard work, diligence, and discipline. The exercise of such usually, though not in every instance, reaps a reward. Erring in the opposite direction to the wack-jobs doesn't correct the problem; it just means we went off the road to the other side. It is a very sad thing that, far too often, we are like the servant who buried his talent in the dirt, and many in the church seemingly have no problem with that, presumably because we've completely spiritualized that text (Matt. 25:14-30).

Ask yourself some very basic and general questions. Are there areas of my life that I can improve upon? Only a complete fool would say no. Where can I grow closer to the Lord? Where is my faith weak? What can I be doing better? What do I need to start, and what do I need to stop? Where can I be a better husband? What can I do to be a better father? How can I improve my performance at work? Where can you improve your health and fitness? What things have I always wanted to do but haven't done yet? Why? What keeps you from accomplishing those things?

You have absolutely no reason to not improve in these areas in your life. What is the alternative? Do nothing? Ask yourself, is that more pleasing to the Lord? It isn't like anyone is asking you to walk on the moon or perform brain surgery. Pick one small thing, one small change, and implement it and be consistent. Your excuses are lies. Ask yourself this: would you be proud rattling off all of your excuses to your children? Do you think they would be impressed? What if you heard them rattling off all of the same excuses for their lives? Your excuses are lies. Jesus said that Satan is the father of lies. It's best not to be found in his company.

BROAD SHOULDERS

Only a Dad

Only a dad, with a tired face,
Coming home from the daily race,
Bringing little of gold or fame,
To show how well he has played the game,
But glad in his heart that his own rejoice
To see him come, and to hear his voice.

Only a dad, with a brood of four,
One of ten million men or more.
Plodding along in the daily strife,
Bearing the whips and the scorns of life,
With never a whimper of pain or hate,
For the sake of those who at home await.

Only a dad, neither rich nor proud,
Merely one of the surging crowd
Toiling, striving from day to day,
Facing whatever may come his way,
Silent, whenever the harsh condemn,
And bearing it all for the love of them.

Only a dad, but he gives his all
To smooth the way for his children small,
Doing, with courage stern and grim,
The deeds that his father did for him.
This is the line that for him I pen,
Only a dad, *but the best of men.*

Edgar Albert Guest

The highest calling of any man is to be a good dad. The theologically minded among us may say, "I thought that man's chief end is to glorify God and fully enjoy Him forever." Yes and amen. However, we may then ask the follow-up question, how? One may then respond by saying, "By loving Him and keeping His commandments." Again, yes and amen to that, but what is the ultimate context that fits within as a man? Fundamentally, where does this happen? Are we to find a nice open field somewhere, or better yet a mountaintop, where we can sit in the lotus position and do nothing but meditate on the word of God? Surely, that sounds super holy and stuff. Or maybe we should spend every waking moment at church; that's got to count for something, right?

In order to get perspective, sometimes it's best to step back and ask some very basic questions. One simple one, in this case, is to ask what man was created for. Man was created in the image of God to have dominion, to rule over the earth. To represent what God is like. He was to guard, keep, and be watchful over what God has entrusted to his care. He was to be fruitful and multiply, to fill the earth and subdue it. He does this through the covenant of marriage and procreation. He does this by becoming a father and ruling as such. Father is the greatest and most influential title that a man can carry.

We call this patriarchy, which simply means father-rule. For a multitude of reasons this term "patriarchy" has become controversial. I would argue that all of those reasons are nefarious and misguided. I would also argue that when something is deemed to be controversial today, it is usually the first indicator that you are on the right path.

There is simply no way of getting around the patriarchy; it is baked into the cake of creation. This is the way that God created the world to be governed. Man is to rule, and this begins in his home, which sets the standard and is to be the paradigm for every other type of rule, or leadership. Patriarchy is the purpose and end for which man was created. Being a godly patriarch is the fullest expression of masculinity that a man can give, and it is also the greatest reflection of what God is like that man can give. Not only is being a dad no small thing, but the cultural attack on fatherhood is, in many respects, blasphemous, in that what lies behind much of this attack is a hatred for God.

Men and women are different. Again, the mere fact that anyone, anywhere, in any way, would think that statement is controversial should pretty much tell you everything you need to know about our times. Again, it should also be a clear indication that you are on the right track. Men and women are different all the way down and all the way through, which also means that fathers and mothers are different all the way down and all the way through. Their roles are designed by God as complementary.

Therefore, to further state the most obvious of obvious statements, men and women are not interchangeable, as many would try to have you believe. Everyone knows this, and unfortunately we are all reaping the noxious fruit of feminism that has been shoved down our throats for decades. The problem with continually kicking against nature is that eventually she will make you feast at a banquet of consequences. We can convince ourselves that we can fly. We can even jump off a 100-story building and convince the world that man can fly…past 99 floors, but eventually we will all come to learn that falling masquerading as flying comes with horrific results.

Come to find out, surprise surprise—contra feminism, dads matter and matter immeasurably. We've all seen the effects of fatherlessness, which are illuminating and terrifying. I will generalize some of the stats here: Those who grow up without a dad present are considerably more likely to have learning disabilities. They are considerably more likely to engage in promiscuous sexual behavior. They (especially boys) are considerably more likely to commit violent crimes and murder. They are considerably more likely to engage in reckless behavior. They are far more likely to be diagnosed with a mental illness and be admitted to a psychiatric hospital. They are much more likely to kill themselves. Boys without fathers comprise 90 percent of those in drug treatment programs, and 95 percent of the cases involving boys in juvenile court are fatherless.

Apparently the solution to fixing our country is much simpler than they would have you believe. All we need to fix every social problem we face today and the massive economic cost that all those problems bring is good dads. It is absolutely true that men cannot do what women can do, but it is also equally true that women cannot do what men can do. It is not just nature that attests to this, but also the soul, of which all the stats attest.

I would imagine that many, if not most, of the guys reading this now grew up without their dad present. I did, and it sucked. There is no substitute for your dad. When Dad leaves for whatever reason, that absence is felt. It is often felt in a home that is filled with bitterness, but more directly it leaves a void in the child's life. They feel alone and vulnerable in a big and dangerous world. They feel abandoned, unworthy, and unwanted. They feel like a ship at sea without a rudder or a map.

One good dad is worth more than 100 pastors, teachers, or coaches in a kid's life. I am not saying that pastors, teachers, and coaches can't have a wonderful impact on a kid's life; most certainly they can, and I would imagine many reading this have been affected as such. Praise God. However, what I am saying is that the daily presence, sacrifice, and love of a father are worth so much more.

This is what I think many struggle with, and if not now, it's probably because you already have or because it just hasn't come yet, but it will. The struggle is, how can I be a good father to my children when I have no idea how to be a father myself? I remember before we had our first child. The world seemed so big, I seemed so small in it, and everything just seemed so overwhelming. I was trying my best just to figure out how to be a man. My upbringing was pretty much shit, and 80's action stars, who pretty much raised me, weren't necessarily the best role models.

Despite how big of a mess I was, God in His grace saw fit to save me and give me His Son. Shortly after I gave my life to Christ in my mid-twenties, God saw fit to then bless me with my own son. The first thing I had to come to terms with was that I had no earthly clue what I was doing, but I knew that God was now my Father through Christ. This meant I was going to have to be fathered by God if I wanted to learn how to father my son. I also knew that I would never leave my wife, and I would never leave my son. Those options would never be on the table, so I had some stuff I needed to figure out.

The reason I share that is for a couple of reasons. One, it's cheaper than therapy, and two, every time I share this information in word or print, guys reach out and are thankful because they have a similar story, and it's nice to know you're not alone. And thirdly, I think it helps to shed light on the above poem and why I find it so awesome and encouraging and why I think you should too.

I have read so many books on being a father and have messed up in just about every way you can mess up. It is easy to get discouraged. I listen to guys that seem to have it all together, and I think, "Man, I suck. I don't even have it half together most days."

Then I remember God the Father. He is the perfect Father. He is perfectly firm and fair. He is perfectly loving and kind. He is perfectly gracious, and merciful, and He is perfectly patient with me and will never leave me nor forsake me because I am covered in the blood of His Son. If this is the case, which it is, then surely I can keep trying, keep improving, and keep going. This may sound silly and overly simplistic, but I think this "keep going" part and never leaving, never forsaking, never giving up, and striving to be better part is part of what it means to be a dad. Sure, there is a lot more to it than that, but that is definitely front and center.

Doug Wilson defines masculinity as the glad assumption of sacrificial responsibility. I believe it was Wilson that also said that God gave men broad shoulders because He intends for them to carry a load. Carrying a load is just another way of describing what sacrificial responsibility is, and surely this culminates in fatherhood.

However, this sacrificial responsibility is most clearly seen in the daily grind, the exercise of daily discipline out of love for those whom God has entrusted to your care. The tired face, the calloused hands, the bad back, and the permanent limp are evidence of a father's love. It's the plodding along in the daily strife, bearing the whips and scorns of life without ever complaining about it. It is even doing all of this joyfully, knowing that it is done out of love for your children. Sacrificing for them is the love of a father. Feeling all the aches and pains and being willing to do it all over again is the love of a father.

As a father, you may never have riches or fame or, according to the world's standards, have anything to be proud about, and no one may be able to pick you out of a crowd. However, the simple fact that your children can recognize your voice out of a million voices makes you a rich man. The fact that your children would run into your arms makes fame seem silly.

So much of what a dad does goes unnoticed: "Toiling, striving from day to day, / Facing whatever may come his way, / Silent, whenever the harsh condemn, / And bearing it all for the love of them." (lines 15-18). However, this does not make it any less important. A father's sacrificial love is like the foundation of your home. It's not flashy, and the vast majority of the time you take it for granted; however, it is what allows for everything else to function properly.

So you can go ahead and read all the books and do all the stuff. I get it, I really do, but at the end of the day maybe it's simpler than we all want to believe, not easier but simpler. Love the Lord and joyfully be fathered by Him. Allow Him to correct and shape your view of fatherhood. Pray a lot. Repent a lot too. Love your wife a lot. Love your kids a lot, and then pour yourself out for them. If you do all that, then you won't have time to worry about being a super dad because you'll be too busy being an actual dad. Then, when we die, maybe someone will say of us, "He was only a dad, *but the best of men*."

DEATH

Crossing the Bar

Sunset and evening star,
    And one clear call for me!
And may there be no moaning of the bar,
    When I put out to sea,

  But such a tide as moving seems asleep,
    Too full for sound and foam,
When that which drew from out the boundless
deep
    Turns again home.

  Twilight and evening bell,
    And after that the dark!
And may there be no sadness of farewell,
    When I embark;

  For tho' from out our bourne of Time and Place
    The flood may bear me far,
I hope to see my Pilot face to face
    When I have crost the bar.

Alfred, Lord Tennyson

As I sit down to write, one day has passed since Charlie Kirk was publicly assassinated at a campus event at Utah Valley University in Orem, Utah. It is amazing the impact that this one event has had not only on our nation but also within our homes. Many have said, and I think rightly so, that this event will turn out to be a turning point or a tipping point for our nation. This is something that we will all find out in the days ahead.

Many are furious, and they should be. This young man had the side of his neck blown out in front of his wife and two young children. Charlie was a once-in-a-lifetime talent. He started Turning Point USA when he was only 18 years old, and by all accounts he was a workhorse. As his friends in the media eulogize him, they mention his accomplishments, but more than anything they are all quick to point out that he was genuinely a good man. He loved the Lord, he loved his wife, he loved his kids, and he loved his country, and despite all the hatred and vitriol that was constantly thrown his way, he never seemed to throw it back.

He seemed to be connected with everyone, and anyone that actually knew him only has kind things to say about him. This is an accomplishment in and of itself. However, at only 31 years of age, he built one of the most influential, if not the most influential, conservative organizations in the world. To see all that he accomplished in such a short amount of time is truly humbling and inspiring.

I am humbled and inspired by his work ethic. I am humbled and inspired by his ability to organize. I am humbled and inspired by his ability to debate.

I am humbled and inspired by his ability to inspire others. I am humbled and inspired by his ability to run in political circles and seemingly be undefiled by them. And I am humbled and inspired by his desire to share Christ regardless of the setting.

It is more than obvious as to why so many are grieving, not only because their friend was taken from them, but also an amazingly talented man who was just getting started. However, Kirk's assassination seems to be so much bigger, and I am not quite certain I can even put my finger on it yet. I never knew Charlie Kirk, and I don't know anyone who knows Charlie Kirk. I am just a normal guy, and honestly, I was really unaware of just how influential he was until after he was murdered, which is unfortunately the way things seem to go.

My family's exposure to him was through videos of him debating on college campuses. So you could say that knowledge of him was simply that of exposure to his work and an appreciation for it, but there was no personal or sentimental attachment. Yet, as we saw the events unfold, it hollowed out my home as if we had lost a loved one. Sadly and tragically, people die every day, and in ministry you are never really too far from death, so the weight of death is not foreign to my family, but we all seemed to uniformly experience the weightiness of what just happened.

I have talked to several others with similar experiences. Perhaps it was because of the public and brutally violent nature of the event. Perhaps it was because many of us saw the video of him being shot. Perhaps it was because he was murdered in front of his wife and two children, both under five years old. Or perhaps it was because we all intuitively felt like an invisible line had been crossed and whatever little bit of innocence that our nation had left was just taken from us.

Maybe it is all of the above, or maybe because it is all of the above, we were all, at the same time and in the same way, forced to come to terms with the fact that life is fragile, precious, and short. It is absolutely certain that all of us will die. The one guarantee that we all have at birth is that it will not last. The wages for sin is death, and we are all born under the curse of Adam. If our lives are not violently cut short, every single last one of us will age out.

Despite the inevitability of death, we do everything in our power to pretend like it's not going to happen to us. Even though it is certain, we are still surprised when it happens. Every single family I have been with after a loved one died all say the same thing at some point, "I just thought we had more time." This is true even when the person who died was in hospice. God has put eternity into our hearts, and when death arrives, it is never a welcomed guest. It always hurts, and though it is certain, it always seems to arrive too early no matter what way it comes.

The irony is, and perhaps it is one of those great paradoxes of life if not the greatest paradox, that the only way to truly live and suck all the marrow out of life is to come to terms with death. It would also appear to be ironic, at least upon the surface, that those who are most focused on eternity seem to get the most out of life and live most urgently in the present. Maybe we can say, at least generally speaking, this is a "*to live is Christ and to die is gain*" type of thing.

To give one's life to Christ, to see and know Him and the power of His resurrection, is to have things put into perspective real quick. To see and know Christ is to see and know that the wages for sin is death. To see Him upon the cross suffering in your place is to see the death that you deserve due to your sin and rebellion. However, to see the resurrected Christ is to see that in the death of Jesus, death died. Your debt was paid in full upon the cross. Therefore, there is no condemnation for those who are in Christ Jesus.

Through repentance and faith in Jesus, His death becomes our death, but His resurrected eternal life also becomes ours. In Christ, we are made a new creation, under a new covenant, represented by the God-man, the last Adam. He gives us His Spirit, which animates our new life and empowers us to walk in step with the Spirit, bearing the fruits of the Spirit. His life is ours, and our life is now His. It is to be lived for Him and through Him and to Him. To live is Christ.

However, this means that death is also gain. What was once our great enemy, through Christ, has now become our great gateway. In Christ, our work done in Christ and for Christ will be rewarded. Upon our death, which is still inevitable in the flesh and is no longer feared, we will hear, "Well done, good and faithful servant; come and enter into the joy of your Master."

So then, even though Christians are given an eternal timeline, it does not lead them to squander, abuse, or waste the time that they have been given, but rather to use it well for the glory of Christ. We can say that our lives are not our own but were bought at a price, namely the life of Christ. There are a lot of things that stand out to me over the last couple of days, and when something so traumatic happens like the assassination of Charlie Kirk, it is very easy to get consumed with anger. No doubt, we should experience a righteous anger that leads to a just judgment.

However, positively, I am so thankful for the life that the Lord gave Charlie and am so inspired by how he used his life and time and how much he accomplished in only 31 years. He is a man who can truly say to live is Christ, and though his death is tragic, his reward is great. His tour of duty is now complete, and he has entered into his Master's joy. This is to take no pain of the loss of life away; however, it is simply to acknowledge the gift of the time that was given and how it was used.

May we all put our hands to the plow, gird up our loins, and live life with all of the gusto we can, because before you know it, it will be gone. Your life and mine are like a breath on a cold winter morning. We only get so much time before we cross the bar. The problem is that we don't know when that day will come, but when it does, we will all stand before our "Pilot face to face." In Christ, death is gain. Does your life reflect that?

See It Through

When you're up against a trouble,
  Meet it squarely, face to face;
Lift your chin and set your shoulders,
  Plant your feet and take a brace.
When it's vain to try to dodge it,
  Do the best that you can do;
You may fail, but you may conquer,
  See it through!

Black may be the clouds about you
  And your future may seem grim,
But don't let your nerve desert you;
  Keep yourself in fighting trim.
If the worst is bound to happen,
  Spite of all that you can do,
Running from it will not save you,
  See it through!

Even hope may seem but futile,
  When with troubles you're beset,
But remember you are facing
  Just what other men have met.
You may fail, but fall still fighting;
  Don't give up, whate'er you do;
Eyes front, head high to the finish.
  See it through!

Edgar Albert Guest

They are only three simple words, but I love them. There is really nothing profound or terribly insightful about them, but they have teeth. I repeat them to myself often, most mornings actually, and at certain times in my life they have even acted as a mantra, and maybe even sometimes as a crutch. These three simple words are "*keep moving forward.*" Like I said, nothing profound about them. In fact, they're not even original to me. I stole them from the greatest movie speech of all time in the greatest movie of all time (that last one may be a bit of an overstatement). The movie, *Rocky Balboa.*

Every great combat movie has to do one thing well in order for it to be great. That is, it has to show that the real fight the fighter fights is always the fight outside of the ring before he ever steps into the fight inside of the ring. It is here we begin to not only understand the character but relate with them, and in relating with them, root for them. We earnestly desire for this character to overcome everything pressing in upon them.

All the obstacles, trials, loss, haters, and so on—we want to see them overcome all of it. We want to see them keep moving forward. We want to see them win. We find ourselves heavily invested in these characters. We begin hearing this primal voice deep down in our masculine soul telling them to keep going, get up, fight, find the reserve when there is nothing left, don't stop, don't quit, see it through to the end, and no matter what, keep moving forward. At this point we are really preaching to ourselves.

In *Rocky Balboa*, Rocky is struggling with his place in the world. He is retired from boxing, his wife has died, and his son is grown and has his own career and doesn't really want anything to do with his father. He is just kind of coasting through life. Everything around him has changed. He still has some fight left in him and isn't ready to move on yet; he is not going to go gently into that good night.

So the over-aged Rocky looks at getting back in the ring with the current heavyweight champion of the world for an exhibition bout. Rocky's son is really more concerned about the impact this will have on him as opposed to his father, whom he believes is crazy for even considering getting back in the ring at his age. He tells his dad that he is going to embarrass himself and him as well. Rocky then goes on to tell his son how when he was a baby, he would hold him in his hands and think about how awesome his son was and how he was going to do great things. Somewhere along the line he got beat up by the world, stopped believing in himself, and became scared and entitled. He then goes on to deliver these words, which again, are awesome.

"Let me tell you something you already know. The world ain't all sunshine and rainbows. It's a very mean and nasty place and I don't care how tough you are it will beat you to your knees and keep you there permanently if you let it. You, me, or nobody is gonna hit as hard as life. But it ain't about how hard ya hit. It's about how hard you can get hit and keep moving forward. How much you can take and keep moving forward. That's how winning is done!"

If those words don't resonate with you, it's simply because you haven't been alive long enough or because you haven't suffered enough. Nobody gets through this life without taking a beating from life. Loved ones die, children get sick, markets shift, and jobs and fortunes are lost; people get murdered and raped—"The world ain't all sunshine and rainbows. It's a very mean and nasty place and I don't care how tough you are it will beat you to your knees and keep you there permanently if you let it."

Bad stuff is going to happen to you, and you have no idea what is coming your way or when. There is no way to prepare for some of this stuff. And depending on what it is, it will hollow you out to the core. We can't control the stuff that happens to us, but we can control our response to the stuff that happens to us. Your response tells you what kind of a man you are and what kind of a man you'll become as a result. It's true that there are things that are so big and so devastating that you simply can't prepare yourself for them. What you can do, however, is tell yourself constantly in advance that you are the type of man that will endure, you are the type of man that will keep moving forward, and no matter what, you will keep moving forward.

Some time back, my family suffered tremendously. It was traumatic. Kind of like someone just shot a gun next to your ear—you feel like you're trying to live life in the midst of disorientation and confusion. Your new modus operandi feels like the cloud of war. I was broken, I was lost and confused, I was angry at God, and I felt like I was left at sea in a ship without a rudder, and when I cried out to Him for help, a thunderstorm came.

In *A Grief Observed*, C.S. Lewis describes well what I was experiencing: "The time when there is nothing at all in your soul except a cry for help may be just that time when God can't give it: you are like the drowning man who can't be helped because he clutches and grabs. Perhaps your own reiterated cries deafen you to the voice you hoped to hear."

I had no idea how my family was going to get through it. Even though I felt so blind, and even though I felt like I couldn't hear or see the Lord and was so angry with Him, I knew He was the only way through it. I needed to wrestle with Him and not let go. "I don't see you, Lord, but I won't let go." "I don't hear you, Lord, but I won't let go." "I don't understand why this happened, Lord, but I won't let go." "I am so angry with you, Lord, but I won't let go." And on and on and on and on…

You may be tempted to ask, did I ever get the answers I was looking for? No, life seldom actually works that way. However, I did get something better. I got more of the Lord and His peace. Someone reading this may be in the middle of the furnace of life; whatever you do, don't let go. Grab the Lord's robe and white-knuckle it. The only way out is through, so keep moving forward and see it through. "When you're up against a trouble, / Meet it squarely, face to face; / Lift your chin and set your shoulders, / Plant your feet and take a brace. / When it's vain to try to dodge it, / Do the best that you can do; / You may fail, but you may conquer, / See it through!" (lines 1-8).

There was a period of my life that lasted more than a couple of years where the first thing I would say to myself when I would wake up is, *"Keep moving forward."* I said this to myself so often that it became a mantra between me and my wife. What do we have going on today? I don't know what the day holds, but whatever it is, we will keep moving forward. It doesn't matter what's in front of us; we are going to keep moving forward.

When life unexpectedly punches you in the throat, there isn't much you can do about it. "Black may be the clouds about you / And your future may seem grim." You can't deny it, you can't minimize it, you can't spin it, and running from it won't save you. At that point, you just have to put your head down, keep moving forward, and see it through. You might make it, and you might not, but I can guarantee you two things either way.

First, if you quit, whatever that may look like given the particular situation, you certainly aren't getting through it. Now, there are times to walk away, and there are times to move on; however, we're talking about times where that is impossible. What does quitting look like then? It looks like conceding your fate, seeing the *suck* as the new normal, and becoming bitter and jaded. It may take longer than you want. It may be harder than you want. As a matter of fact, you may not want any of this—you didn't sign up for any of whatever you're going through after all, but quitting in the middle of the *suck* only guarantees that you will be perpetually stuck there, not only with the pain of the *suck* but also now with the pain of regret.

Second, if you see it through, the pain of loss and trauma may always follow you around like a black dog, but now you know you have the grit and the will to survive. You know that whatever it was in front of you, it did not defeat you. Some days simply showing up is the victory. There is nothing you are facing that others have not also faced and conquered. If they can, then so can you. Life is not about how hard you can hit. It's about how hard you can get hit and keep moving forward. "You may fail, but fall still fighting; / Don't give up, whate'er you do; / Eyes front, head high to the finish. / See it through!"

GAMBLER

Opportunity

This I beheld, or dreamed it in a dream:—
There spread a cloud of dust along a plain;
And underneath the cloud, or in it, raged
A furious battle, and men yelled, and swords
Shocked upon swords and shields. A prince's banner
Wavered, then staggered backward, hemmed by foes.
A craven hung along the battle's edge,
And thought, "Had I a sword of keener steel—
That blue blade that the king's son bears,— but this
Blunt thing—!" He snapped and flung it from his hand,
And lowering crept away and left the field.
Then came the king's son, wounded sore bested,
And weaponless, and saw the broken sword
Hilt-buried in the dry and trodden sand,
And ran and snatched it, and with battle-shout
Lifted afresh he hewed his enemy down
And saved a great cause that heroic day.

Edward Rowland Sill

"The Gambler" by Kenny Rogers, has got to be one of the coolest songs ever. Rogers tells the tale of two guys riding a train bound for nowhere late at night. Bored and unable to sleep, the older of the two finally breaks the silence. The picture I get is of an older guy who is, sagely, maybe even a little gruff, and who has probably earned whatever nickname he has. You can imagine the dim light hitting him just right as to add just enough shadow to add to the mystique. The gambler (the older guy) is somewhere in between Gandolph and Indiana Jones.

The silence is broken when the gambler speaks, "Son, I've made my life / Out of readin' people's faces / Knowin' what the cards were / By the way they held their eyes / So if you don't mind me sayin' / I can see you're out of aces / For a taste of your whiskey / I'll give you some advice." Like I said, the song is just cool, and we haven't even gotten to the coolest of the cool parts yet.

The first thing we should notice about Indiana Gandolph is that he has made a life out of readin' people's faces. This is a guy who has miles under his belt. He has done the work and put in the time. So much so that he has built his skills around being able to read people's faces. This is important to take note of because, let me just state the obvious, this song is not just about playing cards; it is a metaphor for life, which is, in part, why it is so stinking cool. So then, in regard to the gambler, he was able to take advantage of opportunities because of the experiences and work put in. It is subtle; perhaps you may think it's even a bit silly. Maybe it is regarding an old song, but it certainly isn't regarding the game of life.

That is to say, we learn how to play the game by playing the game. Skills have to be honed and often learned along the way. This usually means losing, and probably more often than you are comfortable with. Failure is part of life. Nobody wants to fail, and nobody sets out to fail, but if you are actually in the game (or, if you will, in the arena), you are going to fail often. Here is the thing though: through those failures you actually learn how to play the game, you learn how to read people's faces, you learn what hands to play and which ones not to, and you learn what opportunities to seize and which ones to let go of.

After smoking his cigarette and finishing his whiskey, the gambler is ready to hit the traveler with some knowledge. All of a sudden the night gets deathly quiet, and you can feel the weight of the gambler's words, "If you're gonna play the game, boy, you gotta learn to play it right." Ok, how do you play it right? This is where we are given the best chorus ever: "You got to know when to hold 'em / Know when to fold 'em / Know when to walk away / And know when to run / You never count your money / When you're sittin' at the table / There'll be time enough for countin' / When the dealing's done."

Knowing what to throw away and knowing what to keep is so much of life. This creates so much pressure for men that they are going to miss an opportunity or that they have to have the game mastered before even getting into it. It creates a state of analysis paralysis or can create a failure to even launch due to fear of failure. This ends up with you doing the very thing you are trying to avoid by not doing anything.

The secret to the game, that is, knowing what to throw away and knowing what to keep, is that you have to play the game. The thing about opportunities is seizing the ones that are right in front of you and making the best of them, or by playing the hand you're dealt and seeing how far you can go with it. The real secret, what you learn from playing, is that every hand is a winner, and every hand is a loser.

What does this mean? It means that opportunities are all around us, and we have to be ready to seize upon them when they present themselves, and the more we do this, the more our senses are sharpened for such things. Also, this will help us to see opportunities that others simply don't, won't, or can't see for whatever reason.

This all seems well and good regarding "The Gambler," but what about Sill's poem? What does this have to do with *Opportunity*? Much and in every way. The illustration from "The Gambler" provides us with a vivid, broader context of what is happening in "Opportunity," and "The Gambler" is just cool. The exception is that in this case it is the ambitious young prince who sees and seizes upon the opportunity in front of him, or if you will, he sees the value of the cards that have been discarded.

Sill sets the scene of a battlefield, which again, it is not hard to see as a metaphor for a depiction of life. Here we see a contrast between two soldiers in the middle of a raging battle. The one soldier seems to be on the outer edge, not really engaged. If only he had a better sword in his hand, if only he had the blue blade that the king's son bears. If we wanted to use modern-day nomenclature, maybe he would say if only he was as privileged as the king's son; after all, it doesn't get more privileged than that.

It is important to note that they are both, the prince and the soldier, in the middle of a battle. The soldier has a sword in his hand and every opportunity in front of him to fight. The prince is so engaged in the thick of battle that he is wounded, sore, bested, and now even weaponless, and also apparently without complaint or, if you will, grievance. Given the state of our culture, it is probably best to read that again.

The fact of the matter is that even if the soldier had the blue blade of the king's son, he wouldn't know what to do with it and would find some other excuse not to act. Such is the case with so many today that want to complain about everything. If they worked half as hard at anything as they do at complaining, they would actually find they have very little, if anything, to complain about.

Let me use a general, perhaps even hyperbolic, example, but one that I think still holds. Right now in our country you have two young men, and for our purposes let's just say they have similar backgrounds. One looks at our country and says, "This is the greatest country on earth, and if I bust my ass, I can get ahead and take advantage of all of the opportunities before me. Yes, there are a lot of challenges and obstacles, but there have always been a lot of challenges and obstacles, and though I didn't create them, I can do my part in helping to fix them."

Contrast that guy with the other one who says, "I live in the worst, most oppressive country on earth that marginalizes every group that is not a white male, which is so obviously obvious that it doesn't need to be explained. There are no opportunities for me to get ahead, and the rich get richer, and the poor get poorer, and there is nothing you can do about it. Therefore, we need the government (which obviously didn't contribute to said circumstances) to redistribute all the blue blades, because if we all had blue blades, then we would actually fight."

It is almost stupid to ask which one of these young men is going to live a meaningful life and which one is going to be a miserable wretch. We all know the answer, and I don't know if that was one of the points that Sill was trying to make, but it is certainly plain as day. The prince, seeing the discarded, blunt sword, seizes the opportunity, rallies the troops, and goes on to lead them to a heroic victory.

The battle was the same. The sword was the same. The opportunity to fight was the same. The difference was the man. That is a truth that stings. This is the cold hard truth that many need to hear today. I know this is not true in total, but in many cases it is. Think of the soldier that dropped his blade and left the battlefield because he wasn't as privileged as the prince. In many respects he created the conditions that led to the success and heroism of the prince.

I get it. Life is hard. However, one thing that I know for certain is that it is not going to get any easier sitting around complaining about how hard it is and about how if you only had the blue blade, then you would engage. It is simply not true; if you are not faithful with a little, you are not going to be faithful with much.

I get it; we've all screwed up, we've missed opportunities, and we've all had pity parties for ourselves that no one came to. Ok, no education is free; what did you learn? Get back in the game; get back in the battle. Play the hand you are dealt to the best of your ability and learn and grow from it. Grab that blunt blade and get after it; no one is going to give you a sharper blade if you show no proclivity to fighting. That blade will go to someone else who does.

LOOKING TO JESUS

Disturb Us, Lord

Disturb us, Lord, when
We are too pleased with ourselves,
When our dreams have come true
Because we dreamed too little,
When we arrived safely
Because we sailed too close to the shore.
Disturb us, Lord, when
With the abundance of things we possess
We have lost our thirst
For the waters of life;
Having fallen in love with life,
We have ceased to dream of eternity
And in our efforts to build a new earth,
We have allowed our vision
Of the new Heaven to dim.
Disturb us, Lord, to dare more boldly,
To venture on wilder seas
Where storms will show Your mastery;
Where losing sight of land,
We shall find the stars.
We ask you to push back
The horizons of our hopes;
And to push back the future
In strength, courage, hope, and love.
This we ask in the name of our Captain,
Who is Jesus Christ.

Sir Francis Drake

Marcus Aurelius once said, "Comfort is the worst addiction." This is jarring to our modern ears because virtually everything around us is catered to our comfort. Basically, it has become the life mission of many. We have entire industries built around making people more comfortable. Just think of the pharmaceutical industry; you got a problem, we got a pill for that. Perhaps more innocently, most people just don't want to be challenged or to experience pain of any kind. It's avoided like the plague. No one is advocating for being a masochist, and it's stupid to think that the only two options in life are avoiding discomfort like Rosie O'Donnell avoids the gym or being a masochist.

Is comfort bad? No, not at all. In fact, it is desirable to a degree and within context. In the Marcus Aurelius quote, perhaps the operative word is "addiction." Comfort is the worst *addiction.* Now, we would be fools to split hairs over other addictions that are certainly horrible. Some may be willing to grant the point that being comfortable for too long could have a detrimental effect on a person; however, few would identify comfort as an addiction, and even fewer still would place it anywhere near the top of the list.

On the surface, it seems somewhat ridiculous to even compare comfort to other substances that people get addicted to. When you look at someone addicted to meth and someone addicted to comfort, it hardly seems a fair comparison. Obviously, the physical effects of meth are horrendous on the body and the soul. I am going to sound crazy to some for even suggesting this, but what if compulsively seeking after comfort as the ultimate good and as an end in and of itself is just a more pleasant-looking, though equally destructive, force? Are you even willing to entertain the idea that this is possible, or does comfort already have its hooks in?

Again, on the surface it does seem kind of ridiculous to even entertain the idea. There is nothing wrong with comfort *per se*, whereas smoking meth is always destructive and nothing but destructive. Comfort, on the other hand, is, well, desirable, but perhaps this is what can make it so dangerous. Is it desirable at all times and in every way when applied to your life? Is it good when the desire for it controls you and it becomes the pursuit of your life? What are the consequences of this?

There used to be a saying. Well, I guess it's still a saying. I just don't know how many people actually say it anymore, that is, *there is no growth without growing pains*. This probably originated in the 80s; however, the truth still holds. You can't grow without discomfort. Discomfort and even pain are the places of learning, growth, and maturity. Comfort is pleasant, and we could even say that it is a necessary reprieve from life for short periods of time. However, where there is no challenge, no friction, no conflict, and no resistance, there can be no learning, growth, or maturity.

The very thing that so many people long for and make their life's pursuit is really just a noose around their neck slowly sucking the life out of them. This isn't just true in the world; it is especially true in the church. I'm not entirely sure how we got here;

however, somewhere along the line we became domesticated and forgot that being a Christian, the kind that actually loves and follows Christ, is dangerous.

There is nothing comfortable about being a Christian. People that tell you that are full of crap, or are too busy trying to sell you on the idea of something, or they live in a bubble, or all of the above. Following Christ can be tough, painful, and even messy in a messed-up world. Johnny Cash was more to the point when he said, "Being a Christian isn't for sissies. It takes a real man to live for God—a lot more man than to live for the devil." In some respects Jesus said this much. Well, maybe not the *sissies* part, but He definitely implied it—good and necessary consequences and such—when He said, "I have said these things to you, that in me you may have peace. In the world you will have tribulation. But take heart; I have overcome the world." (John 16:33).

The one phrase that stands out in Sir Francis Drake's prayer is "Disturb us, Lord." Do you want that? Could you even bring yourself to pray that, even if you knew it would be good for you and the church? What do you think would happen if the Lord answered that prayer? I think we could all agree that things would get more uncomfortable.

The American church has confused biblical peace with lack of conflict and comfort. Given this, we are most likely headed for a period where we are very much underprepared for the conflict and discomfort that is on the horizon. Because we long for comfort over holiness, we've grown fat, lazy, and stupid, which is me exercising gentleness. Idolatry never delivers on its promises and always takes away with its left what it promises with its right.

What's the answer? We look to Jesus, the founder and perfecter of our faith. The author of Hebrews clues us in on what that means: "Therefore, since we are surrounded by so great a cloud of witnesses, let us also lay aside every weight, and sin which clings so closely, and let us run with endurance the race that is set before us, looking to Jesus, the founder and perfecter of our faith, who for the joy that was set before him endured the cross, despising the shame, and is seated at the right hand of the throne of God." (Hebrews 12:1-2).

Jesus endured the cross. Why? Because of the joy that was set before Him. Jesus wasn't necessarily rejoicing in the cross, but rather in what the cross accomplished. The cross was the means through which He would be obedient to the point of death, giving up His life. On the cross, Jesus vindicated the Father's holy and righteous character as the Father poured out His wrath upon sin. Here, Jesus also paid the debt for the sins of His people. The Father is declared just while also being the justifier of any who have faith in His Son. Paul gives us a brief summation of what happened at the cross: "For our sake he made him to be sin who knew no sin, so that in him we might become the righteousness of God." (2 Cor. 5:21). Therefore, the joy that was set before Jesus was the glorification of His Father and the purchase of His church.

Enduring the cross and the shame of everything surrounding it was horrifically painful; in fact, we invented a word to describe it, *excruciating*, and yet Jesus approached it with joy. This doesn't mean that we can always see what our pain and discomfort are specifically accomplishing in us. However, in Christ we can be certain that our pain and discomfort is redemptive and that the Father is using all of it to make us more like Christ. All of this seems painful rather than pleasant.

The author of Hebrews continues, "It is for discipline that you have to endure. God is treating you as sons. For what son is there whom his father does not discipline? If you are left without discipline, in which all have participated, then you are illegitimate children and not sons. Besides this, we have had earthly fathers who disciplined us and we respected them. Shall we not much more be subject to the Father of spirits and live? For they disciplined us for a short time as it seemed best to them, but he disciplines us for our good, that we may share his holiness. For the moment all discipline seems painful rather than pleasant, but later it yields the peaceful fruit of righteousness to those who have been trained by it." (Hebrews 12:7-11).

It may sound crazy to many, but we desperately need the Lord to disturb us and wake us out of our comfortable, apathetic slumber and remind us of who we are in Christ. We are far too pleased with ourselves, and our lives and our dreams are far too little given the God we represent. It has been said that a ship is safe in the harbor, but that is not what a ship is built for. Safety is a lie and an illusion, and it is a shame that a ship has never seen the open sea. Thus never really seeing what it is capable of nor what is beyond the horizon. We were not made to be tied to the dock nor to sail too close to the shore. The Spirit that lives in us is not one of fear but of power and conquest.

The irony is that we are dying of thirst while at the same time drowning in the things we possess. We seemingly have everything except for the things that truly matter, and instead of turning around, we drive faster in the wrong direction. We cling to this life so tightly that our white knuckles are almost giving off a transfigured radiance. Should we love life? Absolutely, we should suck every single second out of every single minute, but we should know that we were made for eternity. Only when we set our gaze beyond this life does this life truly begin to matter.

We need to dare boldly. To tame the wilderness and settle and fertilize the barren land. We need to constantly step beyond our comfort, to brave the storms and slay the dragons. We need to stop aiming for earth and set our sights higher. As C.S. Lewis said, "Aim at heaven and you will get earth thrown in. Aim at earth and you will get neither." We need the Lord to disturb us, awaken us, and discomfort us because our comfort is killing us. We need the Lord to give us strength and courage and hope to live fearlessly like our great King, who is Jesus Christ.

Made in the USA
Monee, IL
04 April 2026

47668545R00080